Janet Reibstein Ph.D., Roger Bamber
with Sarah Attle, Jeannette Josse M.R.C.Psych,
and Jackie Wells

THE FAMILY THROUGH DIVORCE

HOW YOU CAN LIMIT THE DAMAGE

Thorsons
An Imprint of HarperCollins*Publishers*

Thorsons
An Imprint of HarperCollins*Publishers*
77–85 Fulham Palace Road,
Hammersmith, London W6 8JB
1160 Battery Street,
San Francisco, California 94111-1213

Published by Thorsons 1997

1 3 5 7 9 10 8 6 4 2

A catalogue record for this book
is available from the British Library

ISBN 0 7225 3493 0

Printed and bound in Great Britain by
Creative Print and Design (Wales), Ebbw Vale

CONTENTS

INTRODUCTION

The aim of this book is to help you take control of your own divorce so that your family can adapt to a new life with the minimum possible pain. Though it should not be a revolutionary statement to say that you and your spouse should be in control of key decisions in your divorce, our experience as solicitors and experts in the psychology of family breakdown has taught us otherwise.

All too often the protagonists in divorce are so overwhelmed by their feelings and by the complex legal process that it is all too easy to pass control over decision-making to others. Often, they feel pressurised into decisions by other family members or professional advisers. But it is the individuals within the family who are the experts on what they and their children want and need for the future.

Divorce is a fact of our lives – Great Britain has one of the highest divorce rates in Europe; in the US the divorce rate is up to 50 per cent. More and more adults will find themselves divorced, and then remarried, in their lifetimes; a large minority of our children will see their parents break up, and a significant majority of these will find themselves living in step-families, with step-siblings and step-parents and step-grandparents, by the time their childhood is over.

While divorce is a fact of modern life, the common perception is that 'divorce is bad, especially for children.' The truth is that, while in almost all cases children would not choose for their parents to divorce, and while divorce, especially at first, is painful for them, it is the *management* of the divorce process which makes the difference in terms of the effect on children. Good management can limit the damage. The reverse is of course also true: damage is increased by bad management – by heated-up feelings, by increasing resentment, by putting children in the middle, by maintaining a battle between parents, and by increasing the costs and suffering.

Matthew and Mary Johnson had been married for 12 years and had three children. Matthew ran a medical supply business, Mary worked for the Inland Revenue. They met at university, married upon graduation, and saw the birth of their first son 11 months later. By the eighth year of their marriage Matthew had had his first affair, and Mary was beginning her second. By the tenth year of their marriage Matthew had fallen in love with a neighbour, and Mary was filing for divorce. By the twelfth they were almost divorced, but still living under the same roof and having stony silent Sunday lunches together with the children. Although two year's earlier they had announced to their children that they were getting a divorce, this was the first and last time the subject had been broached: they had not given any explanation, not given the children a time frame, and not mentioned anything about the new partners who were, indeed, waiting in the wings.

Their middle child, a daughter, always highly-strung and with moderate learning problems, had become over the previous year more and more difficult to control. Finally it became apparent that she was suffering from an increasingly severe eating disorder.

The family was referred for family therapy. In the first session, the therapist gently suggested that perhaps their daughter's symptoms were related to her confusion, anxiety and depression over what she imagined was happening or about to happen (which might have been worse than the actual truth). The therapist went on to indicate that the children needed a clear explanation from their parents about the state of their marriage – what it would mean for the children, why it had broken down, and what they could expect in the future. Both parents, in painful bewilderment, responded 'Why didn't anyone explain this to us? We thought staying together as long as possible was better for the children. We thought not dragging them into it was sparing them. We thought the longer they could stay in the house they'd always known, no matter what, was best for them. Why weren't we told?' They were at sea. Why, indeed, should anyone know how to manage a divorce well? Where *is* there guidance?

It is in response to people like the Johnsons that we decided to write this book.

In the summer of 1996 the Family Law Act was finally approved by Parliament after considerable debate and controversy. The new law, which will not come into effect until late 1998 or early 1999, changes the law of divorce in a radical way and marks a fundamental change of approach. In preparing the legislation there had been extensive consultation with many groups involved with divorce. The White Paper said that 'the Government has received clear indications of dissatisfaction with the current system, and considerable desire for reform.' The consequent change to the law was the official response to the devastation, especially of children, from so many divorces: the new law was conceived as an exercise in damage limitation, encouraging couples to reflect, to co-operate and, especially, to consider all consequences of marital breakdown. This book was also conceived in that spirit.

The emphasis in this book is on you and your spouse having control over decisions within the process of divorce. If you take charge of decisions the consequences will be easier to live with and better than having arrangements negotiated by proxy. It is certainly better than having decisions imposed by a court. It is normal in the midst of separation and divorce to feel so overwhelmed that it would be only too easy to pass control over to others – other family or professional advisors. Sometimes people do so because decisions are demanded too soon, sometimes because of impatience. In this book we lay out the central issues because the ability to consult relevant sections of this book when appropriate should make it possible to reflect, discuss and then agree, at least in principle, on important points. Suggestions given here are intended as a starting point. Guidance about further reading which covers particular legal and emotional issues in greater detail is available in the Recommended Reading List (*pages 179–181*).

A major purpose of this book is to encourage people contemplating or already involved in marital breakdown to approach it with as much knowledge as possible. We lay out the whole story of breakdown, from the emotional process to the legal one, and the interaction between the two. Our approach is different: we meld both together. Both the legal and emotional sides of the story have an impact on the whole family and all its members. The legal and emotional stories also affect each other. Our perspective is that the consequences of the decision to divorce should form part of the decision itself: facing the realities of living apart both in financial and personal terms is crucial to making the best decisions, as is thinking through the impact on each family member. Thus, the importance of a step-by-step guide.

People on the edge of marital breakdown are likely to feel ill-equipped to make tough decisions which are also sensible and farsighted. This is because such decisions are being demanded at a time when they are on an emotional rollercoaster. Intense despair, anger, anxiety and humiliation are normal in the divorce process but do not encourage clear thinking nor sensitivity to others, especially toward the partner on the other side of the breakdown. Yet however difficult separation and divorce may be, it becomes less difficult with more knowledge. This book itself can be seen as part of managing the divorce process. A guide to the whole story should help you to make choices, to understand complexities and to gain perspective. Some information and advice is relevant at more than one stage. We repeat that advice where necessary. You can dip into the book as a guide when you reach various stages of the process.

The book is for the whole family, because divorce is a whole-family process. Our purpose is to help those involved take a constructive approach to a long and inevitably painful period, so that all members of the family can move through it with as little hardship as possible. In other words, we think it is possible, with the help of information and advice, to limit the damage.

The Johnsons are an example of how silence spells poor management of the family process, for the whole family. The Powells are an example of how too much involvement on the part of children can also increase damage. This couple, married for 17 years, each took a different teenage daughter as confidante, thereby creating deep divisions and loyalty tests, and ensuring friction between everyone. Rows moved from parental events to whole-family eruptions. The girls geared themselves up for divorce at least three times, as on three separate occasions their parents announced they were divorcing. The girls told their friends, anticipated the final break-up, mourned their loss. On each of the three occasions the girls woke to a new day, to be greeted by effusively affectionate parents, arms round each other, who promised them that everything would now be rosy. Finally one daughter, fed up, ran away from home; the other grew slowly withdrawn and serious, anxious and overly adult. When the Powells eventually did split up, neither daughter took it seriously. Nor did they accept their parents' new partners. After all, especially since the Powells continued to row even while apart, what was different?

In contrast, Gwen and Rob managed their divorce with a degree of laudable equanimity. Married for nine years, they had one son. Rob went to live with a girlfriend, not far away, while Gwen remained in the family home with seven-year-old James. James' welfare was primary for both. They agreed that James would share his time between their two households, rather than having his main home with just one of them. To this end they had a joint consultation with a child psychologist to ensure that each knew the same facts and shared a perspective on what James would need. They agreed between them ground rules for behaviour in front of James, and about what they would tell him. They also agreed between themselves, with the help of their respective solicitors, about the dispersal of their joint property and assets, and also child support arrangements. They told James exactly what he needed to know and what he could expect from each of them in the near future, reassured him of their love for him, and kept on answering his questions, even though these became repetitive and they grew frustrated with going over the same painful ground again and again. In this book we cover what to say, how much to say, and when, since most people are in the dark about this. James is now 25, having weathered his parents' divorce and a simultaneous and equally divided life in two step-families. He is close to both parents, and on good and warm terms with both step-parents.

Taking the view that divorce is a whole-family process is key because understanding how each family member might feel, what each needs and what each can expect at particular points, can help limit the damage. How well individuals come through it depends very much on how the family as a whole does so.

The new divorce law tries to promote a model of co-operation – between parents and among professionals from lawyers to mediators to counsellors or therapists. Such a model can only help children. It reduces the conflict which we know from research to be detrimental to children. It also offers children an example of adults dealing with issues in a constructive way. This book spells out ways forward in this same spirit. We address when it is appropriate to seek professional advice, from whom, and for what. We also look at timescales: what is realistic and practical, both for separation itself and any post-separation agendas. Indeed, our perspective is that not all decisions need to be taken at once: it is often possible to agree which are priority decisions and which, more far-reaching ones, can be postponed.

We signpost the stages of the divorce process to help not only those immediately involved but also those who help and support them, from professional advisors to family members. This signposting is to show what is normal and to be expected in what will be a long process.

Finally, we want to emphasise the future, the next generation. If the process of restructuring the family is to stand any chance of success, the needs of children involved especially have to be understood and accommodated. They are almost always unwilling participants in marital separation and divorce. If children can be eased through the process then the chances for the family as a whole to emerge successfully are greatly enhanced.

This book is divided into five sections.

Section 1 – The Starting Point: Pre-separation deals with the decision itself. Is divorce necessary? Can the problems within the marriage be resolved in some other way? The consequences of separation are also considered in this section. As part of the decision to separate, it is important to have a clear picture of what the future will be. New problems will inevitably arise and these may or may not be easier to resolve or to live with.

The decision to separate is usually taken by one spouse. How should that decision be communicated? The difficulties of timing are also covered here, and particular emphasis given to communicating the decision to the children.

The last part of this section deals with the practical consequences of the decision, the need to get some clear idea of the immediate legal issues and the early emotional difficulties – preparing for the 'fall-out' of living apart. Particular emphasis is placed upon the effect on children, and the common problems which occur in the early stages of contact arrangements, when children see the other parent.

Section 2 – The Separation begins by considering the legal options in facing marital breakdown. As it may not be necessary to issue divorce proceedings, the alternatives are considered. As part of this section, some of the problem areas are detailed. For example, we examine issues of timing, both from a practical, legal standpoint of how soon one needs to resolve issues such as housing, and also from the psychological one, of how to come to terms with the new realities of separation, as individuals and as parents and children of a separated family.

Section 3 – Legal Proceedings in Divorce covers the legal framework of marital breakdown. It sets out the requirements of divorce, as well as the financial consequences. Both of these can produce obvious areas of conflict; this section will examine coping with the emotional strain of such conflicts. Guidance is offered on how to minimise the impact of the shortcomings of the existing divorce legislation. The section concludes with an outline of the changes in the law and procedure relating to divorce when this comes into play.

This section ends with a brief explanation of how mediation can be used to resolve issues arising on separation and divorce.

Section 4 – Children and Divorce has been devoted to the most pressing issues for children in marital breakdown. As well as covering the emotional effects of divorce, it also considers the position of the children within the legal framework of separation and divorce.

Section 5 – The Post-divorce Family details how and why divorce takes a long time. It begins long before legal issues arise, and continues for most people even after questions of finance and the day-to-day arrangements for children have been resolved. This section deals with the aftermath of family breakdowns as a whole. These include not only the relationships between ex-spouses, but also those within the wider family, including grandparents and new step-families.

This section also looks at divorced parents' decision-making about their children in the post-divorce life of the family.

section 1

THE STARTING POINT: PRE-SEPARATION

1

MAKING THE DECISION

(A) Addressing Problems within the Marriage

In a high proportion of cases, the decision to end a marriage is taken by one rather than by both spouses. Characteristically what happens is that a marriage begins to slide into disrepair and ultimately usually one spouse begins to take action to end it. But though one person may initiate it, the decision is made for all members of the family, whether they like it or not. Often the other family members do not participate in making it. This is especially true for children. It is also true for grandparents and the extended family. Grandparents, aunts, uncles and cousins are normally anxious that their relationships with the children and with the spouse on the 'other side' of the family will be disrupted, reduced and even prevented. Children, of course, worry that their lives will change, that they will lose contact with the parent who leaves, that they won't be allowed to keep loving both parents equally, that they will be forced to move, change schools, change friends and lose contact with their grandparents and cousins. They feel out of control and in the dark.

Clearly a level-headed, all-alternatives-considered assessment of a marriage and its difficulties is preferable to a drift into divorce.

But the problem is that, either when embroiled in unhappiness or excited by the possibilities of an alternative life, it is difficult to see the consequences of divorce clearly. It is commonplace to say divorce is a process that will change things for the whole family irrevocably. But it is true that the process of separation and divorce will inevitably bring with it emotional trauma and stress, and will usually reduce the standard of living of all those involved substantially.

So, the question at the forefront, at the point of deciding whether or not to separate must be: are the problems within the relationship so bad that there really *is* no alternative?

Given the serious impact of marital breakdown for children, parents need to view their decisions about ending their relationship as a long and involved process. They can minimise the consequences of this impact in many ways, which this book will discuss. Coming to a final decision may include the need to seek professional advice in order to make clear assessments about the following:

1 Is it possible to achieve change within the relationship?
2 What, if any, practical steps might be taken to improve things?
3 Are there clear gains from divorcing, and if so what are they?

For legal and financial questions, advice and information can come from a solicitor. It is possible to have a single consultation with no commitment at all to continue down a specific path. To address personal and emotional questions – for instance about the viability of a relationship, or children's needs and responses – consultations which draw on the expert advice and perspective of a counsellor or family therapist can be invaluable. Professional advisors can be crucial in helping people to think these things through.

There are important issues to be considered in making an assessment about whether or not to separate. These will include the following, and again professional advice may help in each case:

Addressing the relationship issues directly, if possible, with one's spouse

Are the problems within your marriage terminal? Can they be remedied? In many cases, people reach the conclusion that problems are terminal without getting any outside professional perspective, guidance or advice. Professional help may be valuable in a number of ways. First, it may help to distinguish 'symptoms' from 'causes' and give a completely new perspective on the relationship.

Where a marriage is fraught, people commonly focus on 'symptoms' or the recurring patterns of behaviour between them. If the symptoms are either too numerous or seem beyond repair, divorce feels inevitable. It can be difficult to focus on and understand the underlying causes of 'symptoms', and most people never even try to discover why they have developed. Sometimes they can be reversed, particularly if the root causes of their development are first located and understood. But even distinguishing between 'symptoms' and their underlying causes is no guarantee that a troubled marriage continues.

A typical example is that of someone seeking divorce stating that the marital problem is the other's 'nagging', which results in increased incompatibility and quarrelling; 'I've had enough, I've just about had it. Twenty years of nagging is what I've had to put up with. We quarrel all the time and can't agree on anything. I don't know when I last felt happy or just at peace. I don't sleep at night. I want out. It will be better for all of us.' This is confusing the symptoms – nagging, quarrels, sleeplessness, for example – with what caused them in the first place. The causes may be either remediable or no longer applicable. Discovering them and changing them can perhaps resolve the symptoms, and transform the marriage.

A consultation with a counsellor or therapist can start the process of looking beyond and behind the 'symptoms' of nagging, incompatibility and quarrels, to root causes. These might be, for example, the withdrawal on the part of one which provokes the nagging from the other, or the fact that one's success at work increases the other's need to draw attention to himself or herself (hence the 'nagging'). Isolating 'causes' gives a couple potential to adapt their behaviour once they understand where it comes from.

When a marriage is fraught, people sometimes feel they cannot even identify specific problems which perhaps they could solve, especially with some help. It just all feels 'too much' and beyond repair. But what a professional often can do is help to separate and identify the problems from the overwhelming feelings. This, in itself, can be a most valuable step.

Another way professionals can help is that through them a couple may find new ways either of coping with problems or even resolving them. In addition, outside help can assist in assessing whether or not the marriage is retrievable. Just as an expert is consulted when one is unsure of medical, legal or financial issues, experts in relationships and emotions can be consulted when unsure about something as critical as an unhappy marriage.

What are my legal rights regarding children, property and finance?

A consultation with a solicitor or a legal expert at a Citizens' Advice Bureau at this early stage can yield facts about the financial consequences of separation and divorce. This consultation can offer information on how to address the housing needs of a family – for example, is the house going to be sold, and if so what sort of property will each member of the family be able to live in afterwards?

One of the most fundamental changes which might affect a particular family after separation is the possibility of having to sell the family home. This is by no means certain in each case, but a solicitor should be able to advise on the risk of having to sell the home in a preliminary consultation. This will depend on the circumstances of the family in question. It may be that there is no alternative if two households are going to be financed – usually out of the same amount of income.

By taking advice, you may also be able to estimate what levels of maintenance would be appropriate, or establish whether the Child Support Agency will automatically be involved.

These are matters which will govern the lives of every member of the family once a decision to end the marriage is taken. Because they will form the backbone of what life will feel like, they should be brought into the decision-making process itself. A solicitor or legal expert will be equipped to give this specific information and may help shape your ideas at this critical early stage about the potential impact of separation, and perhaps allay some of the fears, too.

The most frequently asked questions in these preliminary consultations are to do with the marriage itself. Faced with a number of painful decisions, it helps to know whether the courts have to be involved (usually they do not) and if so when. 'Will I be prejudicing my position if I hold off from making a final decision to separate or divorce? If so, how can I minimise those risks?' These are the sort of immediate concerns that can be discussed with a solicitor, as well as the longer-term practical and legal consequences.

What will be the effects, on everyone, of a separation or divorce on the daily routines, habits and customs developed between parents?

Some help in thinking through these issues may be found through the following:

- *Consulting* what others in similar situations have done: how have they managed to get through the process, and what positive advice do they have? Sometimes just finding out that others have managed can be very helpful in itself. But beware of taking 'legal advice' second-hand. It is important that you discuss your own situation with a legal expert directly, since every family is different.
- *Counselling* to help think this through clearly, in particular the various changes that will take place, so that you are able to envisage more clearly what each change will entail.

- *Laying out alternatives*: what is going to be put in place of present habits, day-to-day routines and customs? Are these realistic alternatives? What are you going to find difficult to cope with emotionally, and how long will it take for new routines to settle down?
- *Rehearsing* what it would be like to be without, for example, the other's help with the school run, or in organising the breakfast or helping with the homework. What will be the practical day-to-day effects of being a single parent? Imagining these consequences and then rehearsing what they would feel like and how you would replace the old routines and habits with new ones can be very useful.

These are questions and routes towards clarifying what at times seems unthinkable: how am I, how are my children, and how are the rest of us going to get through such a complete change in our lives? But as part of the decision-making process, the unthinkable needs to be thought.

The personal consequences of the decision will depend upon how everyone else in your family adapts. What will the consequences be for them? Considering these in detail should form part of the decision-making process as well. The restructuring of a family's life has far-reaching consequences in personal as well as in economic terms.

After such research, fact-finding and questioning, you may indeed decide to end your marriage. Alternatively, you may decide to reinvest your energies, especially in the light of the potential hazards for parents and children in the long process of divorce and post-divorce. Or you may decide you must divorce, but to divorce realising that at each and every step you must be alive to potential damage, and invest every energy you can to limiting it. Looking at these facts as we have suggested above should form part of this process.

Bill and Jennifer had been married for 16 years when Bill started divorce proceedings against Jennifer for 'unreasonable behaviour'.

He claimed that her mood swings and hostility had made most of those 16 years hellish; he saw no solution except divorce. He had recently begun a relationship with someone at work, but viewed that as transitional rather than a replacement. In fact, Bill and Jennifer had separated three times previously and had never sought marital therapy. This time Bill's solicitor recommended therapy, noting how attached Bill still felt as well as how worried he was about the welfare of their two small children after divorce.

After six sessions of therapy Bill abandoned the divorce proceedings. Bill felt that for the first time he understood Jennifer's hostility. Instead of showing her sense of abandonment when he worked each night far past her bedtime, instead of disclosing her hurt that he chose to go sailing in his free time rather than be with her and the children, Jennifer would coldly attack him, impugning his sexuality, criticising his behaviour with the children and railing against his treatment of her. Indeed, the only time this couple shared pleasure was on the rare holidays they took together. Once Bill understood Jennifer's feelings and saw that she needed and wanted him, he felt that there was something they could work on together. Perhaps he could stop work earlier, and go to bed at the same time as she; perhaps they could go out together to the cinema or a restaurant once a week; perhaps he could read to the children at bedtime, at least a few times a week. The couple began to have hope, having separated the symptoms from the causes through therapy.

In contrast, Steven and Marie were also referred to a therapist to see if their relationship could be saved. Marie was clearly so devastated by Steven's repeated gambling, and so angry about his inattention to her over the years, that she had no will to consider the causes and symptoms of their relationship. She had no energy to wait to see if Steven would or could change. After three sessions delineating the problem areas and exploring any possible areas for change, it was clear that Marie was not willing to do anything to shift her anger and resentment, nor to take any further risks; she firmly believed that Steven could not and would not change his attitudes or behaviour. They agreed that they had no choice but to separate.

(B) Who Will Be Affected?

(1) The Spouses

Separation, or the decision to end a marriage, is a bereavement, even if for some it is also a relief. Like a bereavement, it is a drawn-out process with identifiable phases.

The first is largely characterised by *anguish and shock*, including feelings of desperation and denial and a sense that you will never get over this period. Normally this gradually converts to a stage in which the dominant, most frequent feeling is one of *anger*, even rage. Eventually this usually turns into one of *resignation*, and finally *acceptance* and a sense of *renewal*, and the chance to embark, relieved and relatively unshackled, into a new phase of life. None of these stages is discrete – people will usually feel a mix of these feelings throughout each stage. However, most move through the process of divorce, as through a bereavement, in periods dominated by particular feelings: first shock/anguish, then anger/rage, then resignation, then renewal. And most people do indeed move eventually into feeling they can and do have a new life, post-divorce.

We will look at each of the participants and their respective positions in turn.

(a) The Person Leaving/the Person Taking the Initiative

For every player in the drama of marital breakdown, even for the one who initiates the separation or divorce, there is a loss. This may not be felt as acutely as that loss experienced by the spouse being left, but it is a real loss all the same. Once the decision to end a marriage is communicated, these feelings may be submerged under the pressure of others' responses. Nevertheless, the feelings of loss remain and may surface very keenly when others' initial pain dies down.

In fact it is common for the person who is leaving to become numbed to the pain his or her spouse feels on being left. At other times guilt is so strong that he or she minimises the loss, at first focusing only on the partner being left. However, in time, the loss will become felt, for it is real too. There is a strong body of research on divorce which shows that the person who leaves also sustains enormous pain. In the Holmes-Rahe Life Readjustment Scale (a frequently used psychometric scale for stress), divorce is listed as one of the five highest causes of stress. This is so for both spouses. This is because of the huge amount of change, loss and readjustment a person who endures divorce has to undergo, whichever side of the break-up he or she is on.

After 10 years of marriage Carol began divorce proceedings against Alan. He had been alcoholic and violent to her intermittently throughout their marriage, and now was turning his violence toward their pre-adolescent son. By the time she initiated it, Carol was very clear that she wanted a divorce, having already been in her own therapy, then in marital therapy, twice. She increased her part-time job to full-time, moved into a smaller house, and arranged child-care to cover her increased working hours. Alan blocked the divorce in various ways, at first pleading with her and threatening suicide, then drinking and becoming violent, then turning cold and argumentative and deliberately delaying proceedings. Carol worried about him throughout, although in the early period of separation she savoured her freedom. Two years down the line she collapsed, exhausted and overworked, with glandular fever, which then rendered her, afterwards, clinically depressed. The focus of her depression was her loss – the loss of middle-class comforts, the loss of free time, the loss of the once-vibrant love and optimism she had about Alan and herself and rearing their two children together.

Most break-ups are mixed and involve missing the good things, which often remain and might always remain between a couple. First, there may be the loss of daily involvement in children's lives, of the intimate contact and knowledge which close proximity and daily routine can bring if you are not the primary carer.

Secondly, there is the loss of the dream of an intact family, and of the marriage and family life which was, usually, once wanted – the life which 'might have been'.

Other losses include privileges and benefits from your family life, such as access to certain friends and neighbours or to neighbourhood amenities, as well as loss of familiar routines and of security – both financial and emotional.

(b) The Person Who Is 'Left'

The person who is left sustains the obvious huge loss. The wider community usually recognises his or her loss, and often gives unsolicited support because of this recognition. Abandonment without being in control of the decision to end a marriage leaves anyone going through it feeling at the very least impotent, and at worst bereft, rejected and despondent.

Beyond that, this spouse also suffers the same losses as the other: of the intact family, of original expectations of family life, of routine, of financial, social and emotional security, and often also of one's position in a community – certainly as a member of a couple in a community largely comprising couples.

Sometimes the person who is left feels so overwhelmed by his or her own despair that it seems that the person leaving 'has it easy' and must experience no loss at all. This is especially so if there is another person for whom he or she is leaving. Indeed, the comfort of another relationship may soften the blow. The loss is great on both sides, even if not immediately felt that way. However, it is true to say that the spouse being left usually feels additional losses to the one who is leaving: the additional burdens of rejection, abandonment, impotence and loss of control over a major decision in his or her life.

(2) The Children

Current research suggests that from the point of view of the children, divorce is something which is likely to be traumatic, particularly at first. On the whole, children would prefer that their parents stay together, but that they do so happily. This is the rub. Children may do better if this does happen, provided they are safe, healthy and cared for and that they are not subject or witness to any violence or abuse.

It is important to point out that children of divorce can also thrive under the right conditions. The important thing is that the process of divorce is managed so the usual pitfalls for them are avoided. This book should help you to predict what those might be and to look for ways to avoid them. We try to offer guidelines and resources to help make this possible. Most importantly, children will not thrive if they themselves are at the centre, or the object of, repeated parental conflict.

The case of Carol and Alan, mentioned earlier, demonstrates how sometimes divorce is not always harmful and, indeed, can even benefit children. Alan had always found William, their son, difficult, showing him little affection, dealing him incessant criticism and bursting into rages at him. Instead of becoming withdrawn and reticent around his father, William developed a show of bravado and contempt and would deliberately provoke him, especially when Alan was drunk. By the time William was nine, and large for his age, his father had begun to throw him against the wall in rage as punishment for 'mouthing off'. Arguments spiralled out of control, putting William at substantial risk. William's behaviour out of the home at this point also became worryingly delinquent. When his parents separated he clearly stated that he did not want to see his father. Father and son did not meet for two years, during which time William had therapy (suggested by the school) and Alan stopped drinking. At first they had brief, supervised visits. As William got older their visits, though infrequent, became centred around going to football matches every few months. Eventually, with all this help and over time, they got on much better, finding a more friendly and respectful relationship conducted at a distance.

The case of Gwen and Rob, mentioned in the Introduction, also shows how children can thrive despite divorce. At seven James did not want his parents to split up, and became sad and withdrawn (especially at school) for a time and tearful and argumentative at partings after weekends with his father for the first two years. But he eventually adjusted to a new and familiar routine. Because his parents never put his loyalty to the test, always explained to him what to expect, maintained in front of him a friendly, respectful and cordial relationship and facilitated contact between James and each of his parents, James settled into living in both households very comfortably. He had friends in both neighbourhoods, and as he got older travelled between both homes on his own with ease. His school work and behaviour eventually returned to normal. He did a university degree and is presently training to be a doctor.

We deal below, and again in Section 4, with the factors which can help children to adjust well should their parents separate. On the whole, divorce is a trauma. It is one which children can survive, but it is not one they endure by choice, and it has a complex and difficult aftermath for them. If this is not managed well by their parents, the process can leave serious scars for these children. However, so can staying together in conflictual and painful relationships which never get resolved.

This may be at odds with what seems best for parents. If you could coolly consider your own happiness in isolation from what your child needs, it might appear preferable to end your marriage. Deciding what is best for you as a parent in the long run – whether to end the marriage or to stay – is necessarily complex. You are not a spouse in isolation from being a parent. Happiness after the divorce will be affected, for most people, by their children's adjustment to it as much as by the fact that an unfulfilling or unhappy marriage has been ended.

Each child reacts differently to divorce, because of differences in gender, age, personality, life history and family composition.

Nevertheless, research shows that the chief factors determining the quality and intensity of a child's response to divorce are age and sex. Boys are most likely to show overt disturbances around divorce. Moreover, difficulties at the time of and following divorce are more likely to arise when the divorce coincides with a new developmental stage in a child's life, such as starting school or reaching adolescence.

The effect of divorce at each age and developmental stage has characteristic patterns. Younger children are more likely to become frightened or to insist on a reconciliation than are children over nine, who are more likely to become angry about the divorce. It should not, therefore, be surprising that brothers and sisters undergoing the experience of separation and divorce in the same family will differ in their reactions.

When Linda and Nick decided to divorce their two daughters took the news entirely differently. Beth, who was 14 and an intense and emotional child, became angry and vituperative toward her mother and very protective and seductive toward her father, who was moving out. Her older sister, Ellie, a studious and quiet girl in the first year of her A-level course, became even more serious, silent and withdrawn. It was not until her college tutor asked to see them that the couple realised that she had not been attending school for weeks. Instead, she had become involved with a much older man she had met in the park and had been spending her days in his flat with him. The couple had already realised that they needed to discourage Beth's acting out and seductiveness; they had spent a good deal of time trying to modify her behaviour and also talking to her, sometimes for hours on end. Because Ellie had seemed so compliant and undemanding they had not made similar efforts with her. Ellie needed drawing out, time set aside for her, and reassurance of their continuing love and concern for her, initiated by the parents, not by her.

There is also some evidence that children are affected *before* their parents divorce, especially in high-conflict families. At the other end of the divorce process, when it is long over, children can still be affected many years later, the so-called 'sleeper effect' referred to below. This is seen particularly in their difficulties in making lasting stable relationships.

Chloe is a 25-year-old personnel manager at a large department store. She seems cheerful, competent and gregarious. Successful at school, good with money, on the way up in her career, attractive and popular, she has always looked as if she were meant for success. But she feels the gnawing frustration of an intransigent block to happiness. She has never managed to have a relationship survive beyond three months. She says that she would love to get married and have children, but since her parents' bitter and embattled marriage, their long, drawn-out and messy divorce and their subsequent unending quarrels with each other, she doesn't '... believe in marriage. I don't feel I can trust any relationship to make me happy. I keep looking for the fatal flaws and I find them pretty soon. Then I cool on the person and that's the beginning of the end,' she relates, ruefully.

Finally, adult children of divorcing parents should not be forgotten. At a point when adult children are forming their own relationships or are busy with their own young families, they may feel especially saddened and burdened by the need to support one or both of their own divorcing parents, and by witnessing the crumbling of a lifetime relationship on which they have depended.

What children of all ages need at this point is as much clarity as possible. Many children are aware of or sense that change is imminent. If they do, they will need:

- reassurance that it is you as parents who will be managing to sort out the fate of the marriage and any practical issues
- reassurance that (in most cases, barring for instance, cases of abuse and/or violence) the children during this time will be seeing both parents regularly, with clear information about when, where and how often this will take place
- recognition that they will need to be told things repeatedly – even though this will be emotionally exhausting for the parents, and also that these things have already been stated before

- recognition that they will need continual reassurance about both their security and about the continuing love of both parents for them; and also reassurance that they are believed, since their sense of security and the consistency of their world is now being shaken and they will be feeling insecure in many other areas in addition to home life.

In general, all children, no matter what their age, will be affected by the ending of their parents' marriage. This includes adult children. All will suffer, at the very least, a sense of divided loyalties. All will fear the danger of being caught between warring or needy parents whom they love and whom they want both to support and also not to betray.

(3) Other Family Members: Grandparents and the Extended Family

It is not just within the immediate family that relationships change when divorce looms. That decision has a ripple effect upon extended families, friends and the wider community. Telling grandparents and friends once a decision has been reached begins the process of taking it out of the purely private and into the public domain. This can galvanise support for both parents and children, but it can also cut off relationships and give rise to bitterness among former allies.

A couple splitting up usually want and need support from their respective parents. In the heat of conflict before and during a divorce they may also wish that sides be taken. While emotionally important, giving and receiving unqualified support may breed difficulties later on. For instance, if a spouse is cast by grandparents as a villain, children may feel divided loyalties in the presence of these grandparents. In extreme cases, this may make it difficult for children to maintain contact with both sets of grandparents.

Similarly, issues over loyalty and taking sides affect relationships with friends and with children's aunts, uncles and cousins. In other words, a tricky balance needs to be struck between seeking and receiving support, getting advice and help during a chaotic and painful time from close relatives and friends on the one hand, and risking divided loyalties for children on the other.

There is a danger for children that they will become cut off from their wider family. These relationships can be casualties of the process of divorce, perhaps unnecessarily. Yet these relationships might be particularly sustaining for children. Cousins who know both parents might be well placed to be confidantes; aunts, uncles and godparents might provide safe and familiar havens. On the other hand, children need to know that their parents are being supported through difficulties. This ensures that they do not feel that they alone must provide support, and also that parents can maintain as much equilibrium through others' support, for their children's sake, as possible.

Recent publicity has highlighted the wish of grandparents to maintain contact with their grandchildren. This is often especially valuable because it can be a source of stability and familiarity. It is all the more so in the early stages when children do not know whether the separation is temporary or permanent. Grandparents and other extended family can provide a steady source of emotional and practical support and a sense of continuity.

Carol and Alan's children had always spent a good deal of time with both grandmothers. Alan's mother lived in the Borders on a farm, and the children had always spent holidays with her; Carol's mother lived in London and the children, who lived in Kent, had often stayed overnight with her, or went to the theatre or films with her. During the divorce they continued these visits, and William, who had the most difficult relationship with Alan, spent more time with his London grandmother with whom he was particularly close. During Carol's glandular fever and depression both grandmothers proved invaluable: her mother came to stay, and the children went up to the farm for a week while Carol recovered. For these children the continuity and stability offered by their grandparents was essential; when they were with them, doing familiar things, on familiar territory, with people who loved and were comfortable with them, they could relax. They invariably returned calmer and happier.

2

COMMUNICATING THE DECISION

A decision to divorce is only reached after considerable pain and anguish, particularly where there are children involved. Even when a decision to divorce has been reached by a couple, it is often not a truly joint decision. Divorce is a *process*, not a single event, and one person usually wishes more strongly than his or her partner to end the marriage; consequently, it is not surprising that a couple will not necessarily be at the same point emotionally when that decision is made.

One of the reasons it is difficult to communicate a decision to children about ending a marriage is precisely because the couple themselves are unlikely to start from the same point emotionally. As a parent it is only natural to feel upset and confused yourself, and so to be unsure about what to say to your children. Because of this confusion it is sometimes felt that it would be better not to say anything to them. Sometimes parents feel their children are too young and so will not understand. Both these views are usually misguided.

(A) Communicating the Decision to Your Spouse

Communicating the decision to end your marriage to your spouse is at its best painful, and at its worst devastating. It invariably will meet with a response which will be difficult both to receive and to manage. It is best to accept this beforehand. It is important to expect that a rush of complicated emotions from both spouses will accompany the communication.

There is no way to avoid pain. But certain factors can either diminish or increase the painful impact of the message.

(1) The Type of Communication

The more direct and clear a message is, the more constructive. Directness of communication means that it is always better, if at all possible, to speak face-to-face rather than by telephone, fax or letter, or through a third party. Clarity about immediate practical arrangements whenever possible is also helpful. If you have a plan, for instance, for where you can go for help, even temporarily, this takes the onus off your spouse for having to think such problems through at a time when he or she is too shocked or distressed to do so clearly.

(2) Repetition of the Message

Just as when telling children of your separation you need to repeat things over and over, you will find that this will also be so for your spouse. Shock, distress and in many cases denial make processing information difficult, so repeating intentions and plans must be recognised as part of the process.

Patricia and Keith had been married for 25 years when Keith told Patricia that he had been having an affair and wanted a divorce. Though shocked and deeply hurt, Patricia could not believe that he would actually leave. Although she wanted him to end the affair, even more than this she did *not* want a divorce. Because he felt that to leave abruptly and to treat Patricia coldly would be unkind, Keith remained living at home, remaining friendly and affectionate, at the same time that he continued his affair, looked for a flat and engaged a solicitor to draw up a divorce petition. Patricia interpreted his warmth and the fact that he remained at home as an attempt to make things work. When she came upon evidence that he had continued to see his lover she became hysterical; on receiving a letter from his solicitor she went into shock. Each time Keith had to repeat his intention to leave, and explain again that he was looking for a flat, continuing to see his lover, and intending to divorce her.

(3) Giving an Explanation

Giving an explanation, insofar as is possible to put your reasons for the split-up into words, is kinder than just announcing an end. Your spouse will have questions about why, how and when the decision has actually been reached, even if it has been discussed as a possibility many times previously. Honouring your spouse's need to understand is both kind and fair. After all, it is a decision which affects him or her equally to you. In any case, to understand your reasoning is important even if your spouse will not share that reasoning.

Anxiety about a spouse's reaction usually is the single most powerful stumbling block to communicating a decision to end a marriage. This is based on fears that the spouse will say or do something terrible, such as threaten suicide, take the children away, commit or make threats of violence, make painful accusations (some of which might be truthful) and show extreme anger, pain and bitterness. Most people do not want to incur such devastating behaviour or emotions, or to be the target of them, or to feel that they must be responsible for them. People are also stopped from communicating their decision by the fear of how they themselves will feel: that they will become depressed, or that the fear of the unknown will overtake them, or that deep uncertainty about the rightness of the decision will engulf them.

These are both normal and expectable states of fear and anxiety. Unpleasant feelings will indeed accompany the communication. Unstable emotions will become the theme of your and your spouse's daily life. In most cases this intense phase passes, as the decision stays clear and firm. If the decision wavers, changing only to be made and told again, the intensely painful phase returns each time a decision is again communicated. The telling is a deeply painful time, for both spouses; to prepare for this pain by expecting and planning for it, practically and emotionally, is critical.

It obviously helps if the timing of the telling is optimal. Telling a spouse when he or she is ill, just postnatal, mourning a loss, just out of a job, when you have recently moved and there are few supports available, or when his or her best friend is out of the country for a few weeks, will make the adjustment much more difficult. Telling when support networks are firmly in place, when economics and emotions are relatively stable, will cushion the inevitable blow somewhat. Because the information will be difficult to take in, and because there may be questions and intense responses, the telling should be told when there is the opportunity for plenty of time and no interruptions. This must be planned in advance, so that you have a clear time and space, for example a weekend, when children are not around, rather than an evening after work when children are likely to be popping in and out of the room and phones need answering.

(B) Telling the Children

Except for very young children, children need to be told clearly when and if they suspect anything, as most, however young, will have been able to grasp that something is wrong. Most fear that they have done something to cause the difficulties between parents; that, if only they knew what it was, they might be able to do something to prevent things getting worse. For this is their worst fear: that they are bad and that they have let their parents down. They live with that fear unless they are told otherwise.

Proper timing is essential – first decide when to tell the children. How and what to tell them is equally important and must be thought through with equal care.

(1) When to Tell Them

Often children will have sensed a change of atmosphere between their parents at home. They will have noticed if one parent has been absent for a significant period of time, or if there have been periods of separation, or if a parent is spending a lot of time elsewhere. Telling children that there will be a separation after any such periods will not usually come as a surprise.

Having said that, the cold reality of the words, 'Mummy and Daddy are separating (or divorcing)' is still chilling and still needs the right time and space for the children to take it in. As with telling a spouse, parents need to pick a time free from interruptions and long enough to answer questions and comfort intense feelings. As with telling a spouse, children need to be as robust as possible to receive the news. Telling them just before a major exam, or setback, or when they have been ill, or when they have had a bust-up with a best friend or that best friend is away, will increase the damage. But similarly, children need times free of problems, and so telling just before holidays such as Christmas will rob them of that. Timing is a tricky question and there is no perfect time, but children will respect their parents if they feel the parents have at least been sensitive to their needs for support when the blow comes.

It will, however, be confusing to children if one week they are told, 'we are getting divorced', only to be followed in the next week by 'we are staying together.'

Most children will fantasise about their parents getting back together again, even long after the event. If they endure a pattern of separation followed by periods of living together again, then their adjustment to the fact that the separation ultimately is a permanent one will be undermined. It follows that it is best if the parents themselves have a settled picture of where they are going or that they are working towards it, and communicate this to their children.

The hardest stage emotionally for children is just after separation. Both parents will need to give support especially to their children at this point. If they are unable to discuss their children between themselves, acrimony and lack of communication will make support for them much more difficult to coordinate. It is for this reason that, later in this book, we go into some detail on the process of mediation. Mediation may be the best route for parents whose ability to communicate to and about their children is eroded by acrimony.

Mediation provides a neutral environment at precisely the right time, away from the home and away from all the painful discussions and trauma of the breakdown in the marriage. The mediators will help in focusing the discussions onto the children, on their immediate arrangements and perhaps as well on what and when they are told about their parents' potential separation.

(2) What and How to Tell Them

Children of all ages need to be told slowly and repeatedly what is happening. Telling children about separation or divorce cannot be achieved by a one-off discussion. They need to be told in ways that are appropriate to their age, and they need to be told the facts again and again.

If at all possible, it is best for both parents, together, to tell the children what is happening. This fact is reassuring in itself and avoids the difficulties that a rift can create early on. It also ensures that children are hearing consistent information from each parent.

The kind of explanation you give will depend mostly on your child's age. A very young child cannot take in much detail, for instance, while an adolescent will need quite a bit. For a very young child a concrete explanation is necessary: 'Mummy and Daddy don't love each other any more; sometimes that happens to mothers and fathers, though it makes them sad. Both of us still love you; parents don't stop loving their children. Next Monday Daddy will move to a different house, which is near his office, and you can go and see it with him on Sunday. Mummy will take you to Daddy's on Saturdays, and both of these will be your houses.' Adolescents can take a somewhat fuller explanation: 'You probably have noticed that your Dad has not been around as much lately, and that Mum has been extra moody with you. That's because we've been having a very rough time, trying to decide whether we could stay together. We have grown apart so much and the rows have become so ugly that we have both hurt each other beyond repair and don't feel the love for each other that we used to feel. It is very difficult for us to make this decision, and we know it will be difficult for you and that if you had your choice you wouldn't want it ...' You can describe feelings and the feelings they are likely to have more easily to an older child. An older child, however, then also needs the concrete facts and reassurance, such as where Dad or Mum will live, when he will see him or her, and how frequently, for example. For all children, an explanation should be aimed at which tries to stay away from blaming one parent, on the one hand, and self-justification, on the other. Otherwise, a child's loyalties will feel divided.

Yet an explanation which makes some sense is also important. If a child has witnessed a parent making plans to go off with a lover, it would be nonsensical to that child for a parent to deny such an intention in his or her explanation. In general, a child needs an explanation which sounds logical, such as, 'we have decided not to live together because we no longer love each other as husbands and wives should; we make each other very unhappy while living together; we cannot live together without arguing all the time; we can be better to each other and to you if we live apart.'

Sometimes parents have to give different explanations, as they cannot agree on one single one. In such cases some children can learn to live with both, and even, as they get older (or if they are already old enough), have the wisdom themselves to construct a third story, such as, 'Mum and Dad both hurt each other so much they could not stand living with each other any longer.' It is to be hoped that in such cases children can be encouraged to reach this level of insight.

Sometimes having a third disinterested party (such as a teacher, counsellor, or friend) with whom to discuss their parents' different explanations can help a child towards such insight and towards constructing a wise 'third story'.

The following points are also important to remember:

- *Children need parents to create a conflict-free zone around them*, so that they do not have to live with conflict. This is the case even though there may be conflict between the parents themselves. Children function poorly if they are caught in a triangle between warring parents.
- *It is important not to be critical about the other parent in front of the children*, or even to risk that this might happen. It is also of enormous importance not to encourage the children in any way to take sides.
- *Children also need and want reassurance about where they will live.* They are usually very concrete in their response to the prospect of change; they will try to imagine just where they will live, sleep, go to school and when and how they will see their friends. They usually do not want to have to exchange what they are familiar with, and can picture, for something unknown. For this reason, staying at least part-time, or in the short term, in the home they know provides some relief for many children. Emphasising what will remain the same is comforting. Because children need to be able to picture change, it is often helpful to show them what they will be changing to, and also to give them as much choice in enacting this as possible. For instance, if they are going to be spending part of their time in a new house, they would benefit from seeing it, or a photograph of it, early on, and also the chance to choose their new bedroom, or bed, or desk, or decorations for their rooms.

- *They will want to know how much will change.* Will they be going to the same school? They may be concerned that the divorce will not only mean a break in relationships within the family, but also may threaten their friendships with school or neighbourhood friends. If a divorce means moving house, for instance, this could well mean their friendships will change. A child will probably need you to reassure him or her that you will do whatever you can to help these friendships to survive: you will drive them over, you will fix a date for them to stay over as soon as possible. If it means a new school, some advance research and visits to the school would also be helpful.
- Perhaps just as they are concerned about change for themselves, *they will need reassurance and information about the parent who is leaving.* Will he or she be all right? Where will that parent be living? What house, in what street, will there be a room there so that they can stay? Will they be able to take toys there, or other things of their own? Exactly how often, when, under what conditions, and for how long will they be seeing this parent?
- *Most importantly, children need to be told that the divorce is not their fault.* Often children have fantasies that they are the cause of the breakdown of their family relationship. Not surprisingly, they feel very guilty about it. These fantasies can be very powerful, particularly for young children.

All children involved in marital breakdown are going to have feelings of bewilderment, loneliness, anxiety, sadness and anger. Unfortunately these feelings are not always best addressed directly by parents. Instead, research shows that children do best when they have another person in whom to express, confide and discuss their feelings. Often they protect their own parents by not expressing these feelings to them. In view of this, many children of separating parents might be well served by the counselling services for children now available in many towns, schools and NHS clinics, where children can talk about their feelings to people who are not involved.

They may already have a close relationship with another adult, such as a neighbour, or friend's mother, family friend or aunt or uncle. You might consider if there already is someone well placed to listen to your child, and encourage time between this person and the child. There are also pamphlets and storybooks about divorce which you could buy for your child and leave gently in the house for him or her to read.

If possible parents should talk about the uncertainties which their children are facing, and answer questions as honestly as possible. Sometimes children 'code' their questions or put them unclearly, especially if a child feels intensely about something and also if he or she is either too young or immature to phrase difficult concepts or feelings directly.

Children will fear the loss of contact with one parent (usually the father). This will almost invariably be true except in extreme cases, for example where there has been a history of neglect, violence or sexual abuse. Children will want to maintain as full a relationship as possible with the parent who will not be living with them, and it is helpful to have sorted out in advance what the practicalities of that contact will be. Will it be next Saturday, and if so for how long? The anxieties can be reduced if there are clear answers immediately available.

One of the worst aspects of separation is the gulf that opens up between parents. Children are acutely conscious of this and it raises fears that parents, especially the one who is leaving, will someday no longer love them either. Reassurance that both parents continue to love them, even though they have decided to divorce, is crucial.

Alex's story is heartbreaking in this respect, but all too common. For two years after the divorce he had twice-monthly contact visits from his two sons. During these visits the boys were hyper-active the first day, calm by that evening, fine in the morning, and by the afternoon of their return to their mother, arguing with each other and fighting. He would return them, bad-tempered and again hyper-active, to their mother's by the Sunday evening, when she would have the task of calming them down again. The parents' only exchange was over the boys' behaviour, with their mother blaming their father for their uncontrollable outbursts. She refused to talk to Alex and he backed off as well. This frigid distance had characterised their marriage as much as their divorce. The cycle never improved. As the boys got older they found more and more reasons not to see their father on contact weekends – football matches, swimming, friends' parties and social engagements. Alex was deeply hurt, but he rationalised each last-minute change with, 'It's best for the boys not to upset them.' Finally he stopped seeing them altogether, using the same rationale: each time he saw them they seemed upset. He took to spying on them at their school so he could catch a glimpse of them as they grew. They never knew. All they thought was that their father had abandoned them, that he couldn't be bothered to insist that they see him.

Children need to be told that it is acceptable to go on loving the other parent, and to talk fondly of the other parent despite the divorce. It is better for a child to be able to say that he or she misses the other parent and to be given reassurance than to worry about whether or not it is all right to talk about the parent for fear of causing offence. Similarly, children will be very quick to pick up on remarks made against the other parent and may feel these acutely, particularly if they are missing him or her.

It is usually helpful to tell children's teachers about plans to separate. Teachers may be able to help children to keep school at least a conflict-free zone. Certainly, they should know what is happening since separation usually will affect a child's ability to concentrate at least in the short term.

The suggestions made above are of course a tall order. As parents themselves are upset in their own right, and may be confused or angry, it may be helpful to turn to outside agencies for help. Therapy or counselling services are usually available locally for divorcing couples and their children. As has been mentioned, schools often have their own counselling service, or there may be an educational psychologist who might be trained and available to help. The following are additional services which could be tried:

- Child Guidance Clinic
- Child and Family Psychiatric Service
- The local Mediation Service, which may have a counsellor who sees children separately.

In summary, for the sake of the children parents should be as clear and definite as they can about any practical arrangements that will follow from separation.

(3) A Final Checklist for Telling the Children

– Give repeated advice and reassurance to the children about what is happening, and be receptive to their enquiries and perceptions.
– Encourage the children in pursuing their relationship with the other parent, and try not to do anything which might undermine this.
– Reassure them that you as parents can manage your own affairs: that they need not be responsible for helping you. At the same time, give the children plenty of encouragement and reassurance in their own lives and achievements, since their entire sense of security and their self-esteem will have been very shaken.

3

CARRYING OUT THE DECISION

(A) Practical Issues

Once a couple make a decision to divorce there are two important factors in addition to issues relating to children which can make the divorce more or less prolonged. These are, first, the reaction of your spouse and, second, your financial circumstances. In short, the less opposed your spouse is to your separation, and the less the difficulty over dividing the financial resources, the less likely the divorce process is to be drawn-out, costly and painful. You may feel you cannot control either of these, but in fact the steps that you take and the way that you approach the practical issues will have a significant impact on the aftermath of the decision to divorce.

Some practical issues need to be resolved immediately. Naturally, there is a concern that short-term arrangements might crystallise and so affect how things are going to develop in the longer term. Some of those concerns are justified, particularly regarding children. Nevertheless, it is probably advisable to put some temporary plans into action with the provisos pointed out below.

Where the children will be living and with whom is the chief decision for the short term. However, it is important to recognise that it may become difficult to argue later that the children should change their main carer. By the time arrangements are reviewed, perhaps even by a court, many months may have passed and a new pattern of family life will have become established. With this in mind, parents need to keep both a short-term and a long-term perspective agreed between them whenever possible.

It is important to consider what is best for the children rather than the parents when making arrangements regarding daily care for the children both immediately and in the future.

Practical considerations, such as possibly keeping them near friends and in the same school, or whether the parents' work arrangements enable one rather than the other to look after them more flexibly and consistently, may be decisive in formulating children's living arrangements. It is also important to try to discuss between you the possibility that conditions may change as the children get older or your circumstances change. Short-term agreements reflect only present circumstances.

(1) Reaction of Your Husband or Wife

If a spouse is so opposed to divorce or is so emotionally depleted by it that he or she is unable to co-operate, then a divorce is unlikely to be straightforward. It is common to find at the point of separation or divorce that even the most unassuming and passive partners become obstructive or uncooperative. If the power to set the agenda for their future has been taken away, this is understandable. The obstructiveness may not in the best interests of the whole family, but it may feel entirely justified.

Occasionally, although this is less likely, spouses agree equally to end a marriage and there is little opposition from any quarter. Unfortunately too many people minimise what they think the spouse's likely reaction will be, as they do their children's. The logic of this goes something like this: 'If I am so unhappy, then he/she must be as well; if I would like this to end, so therefore he/she must be feeling something like this also.'

This logic is extended to the children. The logic, unfortunately, does not fit.

Human emotions and human responses to the same conditions are highly individual, and one person's response does not usually predict another's. It is much more likely that each member of the couple and the couple's children is going to have individual responses to the process of divorce.

What *should* be expected is that the person seeking divorce will encounter some form of opposition and pain from both spouse and children.

Clarity is essential at this point; indeed, wavering in a decision to divorce is something which is likely to increase difficulties between partners. This is why the decision itself is momentous. One of the reasons the decision to separate is met by such opposition is that it is so difficult to adjust to. The upheaval and the losses are considerable. Adjusting to them takes much time and energy, for the adults involved and for the children. It helps therefore to know what you are adjusting *to*. If there is a lot of wavering, with indications that the decision is not final, anger, opposition and lack of co-operation from the spouse being left are the most likely consequences. To stress the need for this kind of clarity and straightforwardness does not imply that attempts to save a marriage should not be made. On the contrary. It is the seriousness of contemplating marital break-up which is paramount. Once such a course is named and begun it incurs enormous, painful and predictably difficult reactions. It is this that we are emphasising.

Richard and Jane were married for 15 years and had two children, aged eight and 11. Richard describes himself as 'falling out of love' with Jane about six years into their marriage, after he decided she was too cold and distant. He felt himself trapped because he did not love his wife, yet was convinced he would damage his children and lose contact with them if he moved out. In consequence he came to be repulsed by Jane, hypercritical, irritated beyond measure and constantly blowing up at her. She, in her turn, became even more cold and distant, as a self-protective measure. They both doted on and indulged their children. Richard had first one affair, then another, each time believing he had found the perfect woman then discovering her fatal flaw and ending it. Finally Jane discovered his latest love, confronted him and forced a choice between family life and his new love. They tearfully told the children, and Richard left. However, he never really left, as his belongings remained and he spent three nights a week at home in the spare room. Soon his lover tired of this and broke off with him. Richard returned home full-time. The family went on holiday together. But his lover tracked him down and promised him the earth again. He moved out again, only to come back part-time, and the cycle repeated itself. It is still in this stasis, three years on. The children refuse to meet his lover or go to his new house, and they all cry as if it were the first time each time he goes home to his own house. His son has begun wetting his bed and his daughter suffers from night-terrors; she refuses to spend a night away from her mother. Richard and Jane are torn up about their visibly unhappy children, but their indecision is maintaining their children's high state of anxiety.

(2) What to Expect from Whom

As we have seen, children will be deeply upset by the break-up of their parents' marriage. Difficulties *should* be expected; however it can also be expected that most children will adjust, especially if the process is well managed.

Chapter 1 described the losses for each of the spouses upon divorce. Again, this is what should be expected. Both are adjusting to loss. This means there will be much energy spent in adjusting to new circumstances. What *should* be expected is that this is a time of depleted resources, in money, time and energy spent in setting up new lives and adjusting to the loss of the old ones. To put it neutrally, this is not going to be a time of increased goodwill towards each other nor of much emotional reserve. Any extra energy will need to be spent on needy and demanding children who are struggling to cope with their own sense of upheaval.

Another important point which is often minimised when assessing the decision to divorce is the fact that when there are children the couple will always have some kind of relationship. At the very least this is usually a financial one, which can itself lead to anger and bitterness on both sides. When one parent is more financially dependent upon the other there will often be more friction. But in addition, both parents are going to need to continue to negotiate with and rely on each other. For example, they will need to co-operate over arrangements for weekend or holiday visits from the children. The success of these will depend upon the flexibility and co-operation of each parent. Birthdays, holidays and other forms of family occasions such as Christmas or school functions also require contact and the need to get on.

In many cases, therefore, and certainly those where children are involved, it is an illusion to believe that divorce means being free of each other.

(3) Coming to Terms with Each Other's Reactions

It is critical at this stage of the process to keep in mind that each of you has a different agenda. Because of this it is not realistic to expect immediate goodwill or an alignment of interests and co-operation. This will mean difficult and hostile feelings towards each other.

The legal process tends to exaggerate this adversarial position. For this reason it is usually advisable to be slow and cautious about using solicitors beyond consultations for information in the early stages. When coping with feelings of anger and humiliation, it can be tempting to get a solicitor to write an aggressive letter or even issue proceedings for divorce. Whilst those feelings might be justified, involving solicitors at this point may complicate the issues which need to be addressed, and may heighten the tensions. This will make it all the more difficult to concentrate on the important personal decisions, particularly those involving the children.

There are cases, however, when it will be essential to use a solicitor. This is particularly so where violence has occurred or is threatened.

Again, especially where there are children, minimising overt conflict is desirable. The following may be useful in helping calm down potentially heated encounters.

(a) Focus on Practical Arrangements

Practical arrangements are the immediate concerns. Where is each spouse going to live? Where will the children live? When, how often, and under what conditions will children see and have contact with the parent who is leaving? When, how often, and under what circumstances will the spouses have contact with each other? It is essential that these are addressed; the long-term issues, such as divorce proceedings, can wait. Because divorce can be such an overwhelming process, it is advisable to break it down in this way, dealing with the short-term issues as they arise. Taking on the long-range ones can feel crippling and demoralising, especially at the beginning.

(b) Get Advice

Talk to others who have been in a similar position to get ideas on how to manage your feelings, as well as to maintain an overall perspective. It is easy, at the beginning in particular, to become overwhelmed and to feel you will never see light at the end.

(c) Use Mediation

Mediation can take the heat out of the situation by letting trained professionals help you to keep the main issues of finance and children's welfare at the forefront. It can be particularly useful in enabling a couple to move forward through the early phases of the separation and divorce process. For a fuller description of how this can work, see Chapter 8.

(d) Use Counselling/Therapy

Individual counselling can be a place in which you get advice on managing your own angry or depressed feelings, which may be threatening to cloud the main issues of the children's welfare, the finances, and the ability to move on. Many people simply feel they cannot stop themselves from 'being difficult' even though they know they may be making a bad situation worse. Counselling can often be the avenue that saves them, helping them to manage these painful, often valid but also destructive feelings so they do not halt the process for the others and hold themselves back as well.

(B) Legal Aspects

While involving a solicitor too early can be regarded as a hostile thing to do and emphasises the adversarial positions of those involved, it is important to know what legal and practical issues need to be resolved. For this a single, early legal consultation might be invaluable.

One of the anxieties to be faced is the possibility that doing nothing about the legal issues will leave you at a disadvantage. A consultation can usually provide reassurance, and can also point out issues which need to be considered in the short term. The most important questions to address in this consultation are contact arrangements for the children, and housing and finances.

(1) Contact: the Short Term

When a couple decide upon a separation, very soon they will need to face the question of contact between children and the parent who no longer lives with the children. These arrangements can then be presented to the children; they will of course have questions about contact. Although changes will inevitably take place, it is important to tell the children a number of things straightaway. Chief among these is that (if true) they will see the other parent regularly and often. If possible, a couple should communicate to their children when they will see the parent who is leaving and how often they will do so in the future. At this stage, it may also be necessary to consider whether any new partners should be introduced and how and when to tell children about this.

Mediation may be the most valuable investment a parent can make at this stage. Mediation exists to help parents focus on children's needs at a time when parents are intensely involved with their own pain. The structure enables them to negotiate as rationally as possible with each other in a neutral setting.

In the early days after separation, children may have difficulty coping with the arrangements. It is very common for children to get upset either just before or just after leaving one parent and going to the other. It is helpful to discuss and agree a consistent and regular routine for contact as soon as possible. Establishing this as a new custom gets around many difficulties and provides children with a reassuring framework. It is also helpful to the children not to be punitive, increasing the emotional temperature if they should return or leave very upset, but also to put boundaries around it, so that they know they have to find a way to control themselves. Not adding to the upset by becoming emotional yourself and not over-indulging by giving your child the impression that to carry on crying or stomping about will buy them hours of delicious attention should be the guidelines to follow. Sometimes all a child needs is a demonstration of your own affection for him or her and a time to be alone or wind down by reading or watching television, with no additional pressures or demands as he or she 're-enters your atmosphere'.

(2) Housing and Finances: the Short Term

It is important to distinguish between short-term and long-term arrangements in financial matters as well. Both husband and wife have a right to remain in the matrimonial home, no matter who owns it. Neither party has to leave, although it may be best for the sake both of achieving clarity for the children and diminishing pain for the spouse who will be the children's primary carer to arrange for the other spouse to live elsewhere as soon as possible. This is assuming suitable accommodation can be found.

Solicitors often advise their clients to remain in the matrimonial home rather than to move out, quoting 'possession is nine-tenths of the law.' There is some basis for this. If, for instance, a wife and children are left in a home, she may decide that she wishes to remain there even when her doing so is not realistic from a financial point of view. Her husband may then have to take the matter to court, and persuade a judge that the property should be sold. This is a difficult and expensive process. The practical effect of a husband staying is that he is continuing to exert his influence in negotiations, before the housing arrangements have crystallised. However, this may not be in the best emotional interests of the family. Legal and emotional interests may often be dramatically opposed, as here.

Agreeing mutually for one spouse to move out temporarily, and recording that agreement, would achieve a more protected solution. It helps to explain your intentions in case of a later disagreement, and in particular about whether the arrangement was a permanent one. If such a dispute ever does have to be resolved by a court, the judge is not legally required to follow that agreement, but it is helpful for the judge to understand the background.

Clearly, these considerations do not apply if there is violence. If either party is the subject of violence, or is threatened with it, solicitors should be informed immediately. It is possible to get emergency orders from the court to protect families from domestic violence.

If maintenance payments are made these too should be recorded as short term, without prejudice to the levels of long-term support. Otherwise there could easily be a disagreement about what is adequate or affordable on a permanent basis. That would, for example, be unfair to a spouse who has moved into inadequate or expensive short-term accommodation. It is also easy to misgauge appropriate amounts of support early on, for it is likely to take time for expenditure to settle into a new regular pattern.

Separate banking may be another step to take at this stage in the process. In sorting out these arrangements, clarity about who is responsible for which debts or outgoings is necessary, including any charge cards.

It may also be possible at this early point to keep a joint account running to handle the existing standing orders, if this can be done without serving as a source of conflict. Flexibility is helpful early on until each spouse gets a clearer picture of what his or her individual operating expenses will be. However, there are risks involved. If there is a possibility that your spouse is going to run up debts or withdraw large sums of money, then having a joint account could prejudice your priorities. You might be left with having to pay. If there is a danger of this, you should talk it through with your solicitor. Much depends on how much you can agree with and how much you can ultimately rely on each other. The more you can do so, the better.

If short-term arrangements can be established early there is less risk of the larger issues, such as the family's capital, getting out of hand later. Discussions about money and children will keep arising over the years. The importance of getting into the habit, early, of discussing things without acrimony cannot be overstated. If it is possible to negotiate your way through these early issues, there will be a framework and a basis for optimism about negotiations in the future. But if mistrust creeps in early, the likelihood is that it will get worse, souring relationships and making further discussion more difficult. Financial matters are never remote from emotional ones. The threat of financial discussions becoming heated and bitter is always imminent.

As finances are often the source of arguments at this and later points, again mediation may be helpful in keeping discussions about them rational and practical.

As a general rule, if it is not possible to agree on an issue in the early stages, couples should leave it until it is possible to take it to mediation or to consider it with solicitors.

section 2

THE SEPARATION

4

THE LEGAL ASPECTS OF SEPARATION

(A) To Divorce or Not to Divorce

To divorce or not is a question which looms large immediately after separation. Often it can be the central one, causing considerable anxiety and concern. As time goes on, the question of whether to end the marriage formally usually becomes less and less important. Instead, couples eventually get to the stage of agreeing to it as part of resolving various other issues to do with financial settlements and arrangements for the children.

Under the new law of divorce (Family Law Act 1996) it will not be possible to apply for a divorce until a period of 12 to 15 months has passed following an initial information session. Indeed, the party who initiates the divorce does not have to distinguish whether there should be a divorce or a separation order until after that period. This procedure will do much to defuse the early anxieties. But this law will probably not be introduced in practice until late 1998 or early 1999. The features of the new law – and its clear advantages – are described in Chapter 7.

Unfortunately, under the current law of divorce, to start divorce proceedings immediately you have to give detailed evidence of your spouse's adultery or unreasonable behaviour. The requirement to give such evidence usually antagonises what is already a difficult situation. The alternative is to wait for a period of at least two years' separation to elapse. Many husbands and wives do not want to issue proceedings, but they often feel acutely concerned that they will be left at a disadvantage if they do not. Psychologically, keeping or regaining the initiative carries considerable weight. In the emotional context already described, this is no surprise.

Even under the current law, a 'quickie' divorce is likely to take around six months, and possibly longer depending on a number of factors such as how busy the particular court is or whether your spouse opposes the divorce.

The Disadvantages of Divorcing Early On

If one or other party launches into divorce proceedings, inevitably there will be an emotional backlash. It is easy to overlook the fact that the marriage is something that belongs to both husband and wife, regardless of who has done what. Immediately adversarial positions become firmer: attitudes will become more entrenched. If this happens before sensitive issues regarding parenting are dealt with, then negotiations may be undermined.

As will be seen in Chapter 7, court proceedings have their own timetables and these will often jar with the emotional process of divorce.

It is relatively easy for either party to issue proceedings. With proceedings comes the question of costs: who should pay for those proceedings? For example, if a wife issues proceedings against her husband because of his unreasonable behaviour, she can ask him to pay for the costs of issuing divorce proceedings. These can be modest relative to the costs of sorting out financial negotiations, which are separate, but a bill for more than £300 to £500 is still not insubstantial.

The alternative is to negotiate how much should be paid by each, and this may reduce, if not eradicate, this source of tension.

Issuing divorce proceedings without agreement is likely to be seen as a hostile thing to do. Despite this, it is still common for people to file proceedings at the court without warning the other spouse, either out of a sense of anger or from anxiety at losing the initiative.

The Code of Practice of the Solicitors Family Law Association (*see Chapter 9*) recommends that a draft divorce petition be sent to the other spouse, or to his or her solicitor, before being finalised and sent to the court. This enables the other spouse to have a say in the content of the petition, and also provides an opportunity for him or her to agree about who will pay for the cost of the divorce. This whole area is discussed in more detail in Section 3.

In cases in which there is violence, divorce proceedings may often be issued immediately. That apart, the one advantage of issuing proceedings is that you can then ask the court to help in adjudicating over matters relating either to the children, if that is necessary, or more commonly to finance and property. Even so, most couples prefer to try to discuss matters first, *before* issuing proceedings.

Many people prefer, if at all possible, to postpone the question of divorce as a separate issue, so that it does not colour discussions about children or practical arrangements for their separate futures.

For this reason alone it is probably helpful in the early stages to agree not to issue proceedings. This can be done perhaps through solicitors, by correspondence, if they are instructed. It may be necessary, however, to agree to a future date to review when divorce proceedings might begin.

(B) What Are the Alternatives to Issuing Divorce Proceedings?

(1) Deed of Separation

When couples are able to negotiate about children and financial matters, it is possible to record the details in a formal way. It is not necessary to go to court for an order. The terms can be set out in a Deed of Separation, which would normally be prepared by a solicitor. This could record either short-term or longer-term arrangements, or even a mixture of the two.

The Deed might, for example, state the fact that the couple prefer to wait for two years before issuing divorce proceedings. It is not possible to be contractually bound by such a promise, but it is a statement of intention.

The Deed can also record any maintenance agreements between spouses, even if these are only on an interim basis. It is possible to claim a limited amount of income tax relief where maintenance is paid from one spouse to the other, for themselves or for the benefit of children.

The position of the Child Support Act complicates maintenance that is paid for children. This is dealt with in Chapter 5.

The most thorny financial matter is usually the family home. Even if the longer-term questions of whether it is to be sold and how the proceeds are to be divided cannot be resolved, a Deed of Separation can at least record an interim position and the fact that the current arrangement is only a temporary one.

However, it is quite common for a Deed of Separation to contain all the terms of a financial settlement. The Deed can also state that when divorce proceedings are finally issued, for instance after two years, these terms will be incorporated into a court order confirming them.

Even if the agreement contained in a Deed of Separation is intended to be final, it is possible for a court to alter it. Courts, though, are reluctant to do this, especially if each spouse has provided details of his or her financial position (*see Chapter 5*) and has taken separate legal advice. If the couple intend the settlement to be final, it is important for each to know that the issues cannot be reopened.

(2) Judicial Separation

It is possible to ask a court to recognise formally that a separation has taken place in a process called judicial separation. The husband and the wife remain married but are 'judicially separated'. This is not very commonly used as a procedure, though it is an attractive option for those who object to divorce on religious grounds.

Obtaining a decree of judicial separation from the court effectively suspends the marriage. As the marriage still exists, the widow's or widower's pension rights may still remain open. This can be particularly important for those divorcing in later years.

The procedure, though, is essentially the same as divorce. Evidence of adultery, unreasonable behaviour or desertion will be necessary, unless the couple are prepared to wait for two years or have already been separated for five years.

Another advantage of judicial separation proceedings is that the court can adjudicate upon any aspect (relating to finances or perhaps the children) that cannot be agreed, but without a full divorce taking place.

Under the new law, it is proposed that the court will be able to make a separation order as an alternative to a divorce order. The decision of which alternative to choose need not be made until after the period of reflection and consideration.

(3) Other Proceedings

It is possible to obtain from the court orders for maintenance, without the issue of divorce proceedings.

There is also the alternative of the Child Support Agency, if money is not being paid for children or the appropriate sum cannot be agreed. In certain circumstances, the Child Support Agency will become involved in any event (see Chapter 5 for a discussion of this).

5

THE FINANCIAL ASPECTS OF SEPARATION

In practical terms, often the most difficult area to resolve is the family's finances. Though it need not be, this is the most common battleground.

For most families the process of separation involves taking unpalatable decisions about money. Inevitably there are two households to fund and resources are stretched to an extent that may be impossible to anticipate. It is tempting to make snap decisions about money. It is more helpful to assemble all the information and lay the financial options out for full consideration. This can be done between the couple, but in the immediate aftermath of separation this is usually difficult to do without disagreement.

Instead, couples may find it more constructive to take questions about finances to mediation, to negotiate them in a neutral setting. In this way, the couple can be helped to focus on the important issues, and negotiations are then more constructive. Alternatively, the couple may prefer to instruct solicitors to negotiate on their behalf, or there could be a mixture of both legal advice and mediation. This is considered in Chapter 8.

Whichever method is used for discussing financial arrangements, the same ground rules apply. It is therefore helpful to know and understand the legal framework since this will determine the shape of negotiations and the ultimate settlement. Whether the couple wish to have the financial settlement expressed in a Deed of Separation or in a court order, the issues are the same, and a comprehensive settlement will have the same elements.

Ultimately, it is necessary to consider what orders a court might make. This is for two reasons.

First, if the settlement leaves out one of the types of order that a court can make, then the right to make an application for that order may remain open. The settlement will therefore be incomplete. For example, if a Deed of Separation only deals with maintenance, and does not look at the capital issues, then it cannot be regarded as a final settlement. It will be possible for one or other spouse to make a further application later for the capital to be dealt with. Even if one type of order is not needed to carry out the wishes of the couple, it should be agreed that the right to make such an application will be dismissed.

Deeds of Separation are often drafted with the final order incorporated so that this can ultimately be presented to the court. This is particularly helpful for couples who are waiting two years to divorce following their initial separation.

Secondly, the approach of the court is the ultimate yardstick for any negotiations. If one spouse feels that the settlement is unfair, then he or she will take the matter through to court and ask a judge to resolve the financial issues.

For example, it may be that negotiations in mediation have come to a halt because a husband refuses to allow some savings in his name to be used towards the purchase of a house. The wife on the advice of her solicitor may be told that the court would almost certainly order the assets to be used to purchase a house, because of the particular circumstances of that case. The wife in these circumstances would probably not accept a settlement which omitted these savings, knowing that a court would probably deal with these assets differently.

In the end, the court decides what is fair, even if presented with an application for an order to be made by agreement. It is therefore important to know how a court deals with issues of finance.

(A) What Orders Can a Court Make?

Courts are given by Parliament a menu of orders which can be made. The courts are usually restricted to making these orders but, as will be seen, their powers are very considerable and flexible. The orders between possible spouses are these:

- *an order for maintenance*: either party can be ordered to pay maintenance, and an interim order can be obtained if that is necessary: the right to claim maintenance potentially continues until the person receiving it remarries or dies – (*see also below: 'The Clean Break Settlement'*);
- *an order for a lump sum*: as with all orders, it can be against either party, to pay a sum of money to the other (usually as a single payment, but possibly as a payment by instalments);
- *an order to transfer property*: either spouse can be asked to transfer all or any of his or her assets or property, whether these are owned jointly or individually;
- *an order to sell property and divide the proceeds*: this is usually applied to houses, and additional orders can be made, as for the repayment of mortgages and professional fees out of the proceeds as well as the apportionment of the net proceeds between the couple involved;
- *a power to vary trusts made between spouses*: this is not invoked very often, but may be used in the difficult area of pensions.

Where a Petition is sent to the court after 1st July 1996, the court can order maintenance or the lump sums that may be available to be paid direct from any pension scheme in which one or other spouse has a benefit.

The court can only make one order dealing with capital – all the orders above except that for maintenance. Maintenance can always go up or down and a court can always vary it so long as the right to maintenance has not been dismissed. A variation may be appropriate if the circumstances of either party changes.

(Potentially, the instalments of a lump sum can also be varied, but this is rare.)

When the Family Law Act 1996 comes into force, courts will be able to make additional capital orders when orders for maintenance come to be varied. For example, if a couple have divorced and had their main capital settlement, but the husband as part of that settlement is ordered to pay maintenance to his wife, then she can apply for a further capital sum to be paid to her when she asks for the maintenance to be reviewed and varied. This is an exception to the general position set out above.

These are the orders that a court can make in relation to one spouse as against another spouse. It is also possible to ask the court to make orders in favour of children, for maintenance or for a lump sum. However, the impact of the Child Support Act means that the question of maintenance for children has to be considered under separate rules. These are dealt with at the end of this chapter.

(B) What Approach Does the Court Take?

Before the court makes any of these orders, it has to look at a check-list of considerations. These are set out in Section 25 of the Matrimonial Causes Act 1973, which is the main legislation dealing with divorce and finance. These considerations are very much what one would expect the court to have to bear in mind when balancing the financial needs of the parties. Below we set out the main ones.

(1) The Children's Needs

The first consideration is what the children need, including what level of income is necessary to run a household (but see the section on the Child Support Act below) and also where they will live.

(2) Husband's and Wife's Needs

Most of the ensuing discussion will centre on what level of income is needed for each spouse, and how much capital is needed to house them. In balancing these needs it will be necessary to analyse expenditures in some detail; the mechanics of this are considered below. Part of this area of discussion will also centre on the house and the question of where each spouse will live in the future. Will it be possible to afford to keep the current family home going and to run another household as well; or will the family home need to be sold?

(3) Financial Resources

A great deal of the early part of any discussions will be an examination of the family's financial resources. These may include properties, for example the family home as well as any savings there are in building society accounts or shares. (*See 'Financial Information', below.*) Financial resources are not only those actually in existence. The examination of financial resources goes beyond this to potential areas of capital and income now and in the future. How much can either spouse borrow from a building society to buy a property? To what extent can the family's overall earnings be increased, and what about pensions and potential inheritances?

(4) The Age of the Parties

A spouse who is over 50 has very different needs and expectations from somebody who is in his or her twenties, and this is taken into account by the courts.

(5) Duration of the Marriage

The courts will treat a short marriage, of say a year or two, rather differently from one that has been in existence for 10 or 20 years.

(6) Contributions, including to the Welfare of the Family

Contributions are construed more broadly than direct financial ones. Generally speaking, somebody who has brought up the children rather than working outside the home will be considered as having contributed as much to the marriage as the other spouse who may have been the main breadwinner.

(7) Pensions and Loss of Widow's Benefits

This is a complicated area, and for this reason specific legal advice should be taken about it. One problem is that occupational pensions cannot yet be divided; it is intended that new legislation will be available to split pensions such as these in the future, though it is not anticipated that this will come into effect until the year 2000. Occupational pension schemes affect very many families, and their capital worth can be substantial.

Divorced women who have not made significant contributions to their own individual pension schemes are greatly disadvantaged. There is a danger that they will remain financially vulnerable in the future. This area is dealt with in more detail under 'Potential Legal Issues about Finance: Pensions and Life Assurance', below.

(C) Financial Information ('Disclosure')

Before any financial discussions can start properly it is necessary to gather together all relevant financial information, including assets and liabilities, income and expenditures. This process is necessary whether or not the couple go to mediation, discuss the division of assets between solicitors, or issue proceedings through the courts in full-scale financial proceedings. This process of giving financial information is sometimes called 'disclosure'.

Each spouse has a legal duty to give full financial information to the other. Feelings, especially over questions of fairness, can get in the way of financial discussions. By giving a complete financial picture and being straightforward in answering financial enquiries, each spouse can help to reduce potential emotional stress and hostility stemming from fear of concealment or dishonesty.

It is not possible to negotiate the financial issues, especially the longer-term ones, until this process is complete. Sometimes this can lead to frustration, with one spouse and his or her solicitor repeatedly requesting additional information, sometimes of quite a detailed nature. Nonetheless, this is an important stage which cannot be rushed if relevant financial information remains to be disclosed. Everyone must be put fully in the picture, to know precisely what the family needs and resources are before considering how to reallocate them and before constructive discussions can begin. To begin this process, couples first have to work out their respective budgets.

(1) Budgets

Each spouse will need to compile detailed budgets of what his or her likely expenses and income will be. These will probably undergo a number of changes in the early stages, as it is difficult to know precisely how much these will be – especially expenses – following a change in households.

(2) Financial Documentation

It is usual to provide supporting documents to back up information provided. This means providing at least the following:

- six months' bank statements and tax form P60;
- details of how much is outstanding on the mortgage (a redemption statement);
- details of any life assurance policies, and in the case of endowment policies full details of the surrender value of the policy and what benefits will be available on maturity;

- a list of bank and building society accounts, including a recent statement or a copy of the passbook;
- details of any pension benefits, including the transfer value of the pension, and in the case of occupational pensions a copy of the rules of the pension scheme;
- details of any shares or other savings, with a copy of any share portfolio valuation from the broker;
- details of all properties, including those owned with third parties, holiday homes, time shares as well as the main home itself;
- details of all debts and liabilities, whether in joint names or in the name of one spouse only.

In working out a family's resources, valuations may have to be prepared for the home and any other properties. This can be an expensive process and it may be helpful to discuss with a solicitor whether such a valuation might be prepared on a joint basis, with both spouses sharing the expense.

In the case of more affluent families, additional details and documentation will need to be provided, particularly about any family businesses, family trusts, or membership of Lloyds.

For some people, especially those who are not used to dealing with finance, the process of disclosure can be bewildering. It can aggravate considerably feelings of despair or rejection, especially if one spouse is less used to dealing with money matters. When feelings do intrude and prevent you from dealing competently with financial issues, it can be helpful to note your questions and take them to your next meeting with your solicitor.

If both parties are going to negotiate on an equal footing, the process of disclosure has to include not only a supply of information, but also time for both spouses to understand it fully. Decisions in these negotiations will have an impact on the well-being of the whole family long into the future. A settlement which has not been thought through, or which is based upon inadequate information, will undermine everybody and can also sow seeds for future bitterness.

(D) Potential Legal Issues about Finance

The financial needs and resources of each family are unique. One of the great advantages of the legal framework is that it is very adaptable. The exception to this is the Child Support Act, which is referred to later on in the book.

It is impossible to predict what the particular concerns of any one family will be. However, there are a number of issues that are so common that we deal with them in some detail.

(1) Maintenance

Immediately after separation but preferably as a prelude to it, the couple should work out how best to meet financially the day-to-day needs of family members. For some these considerations can be postponed, with things kept going as they are by maintaining a joint bank account. Much depends upon the degree of trust and understanding about money matters between the husband and wife.

Establishing as soon as possible what level of maintenance needs to be paid must be a top priority. If a mother with young children is left in the family home, for instance, she will wish to know immediately how much money she will be allowed each month, to provide food, clothing and other needs for herself and her children. Similarly, her husband will need to know how much he has left over to feed and clothe himself, and to provide for his children during the times they will be with him.

With *interim* maintenance (the sums paid initially, before a final settlement) there will be a good deal of trial and error. A first step in this interim process is to establish what have been the typical housekeeping bills. With many couples, usually one person has dealt with the family's finances. Now both will have to do so. This requires patience towards the spouse who is not used to dealing with money, and who may be anxious about learning to manage finances, perhaps for the first time. Managing family finances is a real skill which does need to be acquired through practice. In addition, coming to terms with diminished resources, which is the truth for most families who split into two households, is hard for everybody in the family at this stage.

There are two basic components in working out maintenance: first how much is needed, and second how much can be afforded when balanced against the needs of the payer.

Where children are involved, maintenance will be apportioned between the parent receiving maintenance and the children themselves. Legal advice on this question should be taken, since the solution may have a bearing on future maintenance levels and may have an impact upon any Child Support Act calculation.

(2) For How Long Should Maintenance Be Paid?

'The Clean Break' Settlement

Potentially, maintenance is payable until the person receiving it remarries or dies. This will not be appropriate after a short marriage, or when a couple are still quite young.

For many families, for example in families in which a mother looks after young children, maintenance needs to be paid on a long-term basis. When maintenance is paid on an open-ended basis, the sum paid may be reviewed. Maintenance can be varied upwards or downwards, depending upon circumstances.

If there is a court order in place, or if one is contemplated, the court is under a duty to consider whether or not a 'clean break' is possible. This means that it considers whether it is feasible to stop maintenance for both spouses.

Children's maintenance, as opposed to a spouse's, will always have to be paid as long as they are dependants. Children's maintenance can never be dismissed.

A spouse does not have to be maintained for ever. A 'clean break' means that a settlement can be reached which enables both spouses to be self-sufficient. This may entail a capital sum being paid over, for example to a wife who otherwise would not be able to make ends meet. Alternatively, the lump sum may be invested for the future rather than for the present, to supplement the State Pension.

The advantage of this is that spouses are free of continual negotiation with each other over future maintenance; they are more financially independent of each other, and uncertainty about finances between them in the future is substantially reduced.

Realistically, a spouse's maintenance can only be dismissed if it is possible for him or her to be self-sufficient. To a certain extent this will depend upon how any capital has been distributed. For example, if a mother who is not earning a separate income is left to pay a mortgage which she cannot manage on her own, she will probably need to continue to be maintained. A clean break will not be possible.

In addition, even if it is possible to be self-sufficient in the short term, it may still be necessary to ask about the long term. For instance, it may be possible for a non-working or low-earning mother to sustain herself and her children on child maintenance, single-parent benefit and child benefit. However, it might not be possible then for her to make any contribution to a necessary pension for her future, when she will no longer have child maintenance and parental benefits.

For example, if the money from all these sources amounts to, say, £12,000 a year, this might just be enough to keep the household going with enough money for the mother and the children. But when the child maintenance stops after the children have left school, although the income may still be enough to meet the day-to-day needs, it may not be enough to make the substantial contributions that will be necessary to build up a pension fund for the future.

Even if a clean break is not possible straightaway, there is a potential middle course. A court can make an order that maintenance should be paid for a specific number of years. This can allow, for example, a wife to retrain in order to rebuild her own career. In addition, it is possible for a court to direct that the period of maintenance cannot be extended. There are, therefore, four types of order that can be made, as follows:

(i) *An order for open-ended maintenance.* This is payable until the person receiving it remarries or dies. It can always be varied up or down, depending upon any change in circumstances. On variation the court still has a duty to consider the possibility of the maintenance being dismissed entirely.
(ii) *An order for maintenance for a specified period, which can be extended.* This can be varied in two ways: it can be varied as to the amount of maintenance being paid, as under an open-ended maintenance order, or it can be varied as to the length of time for which it should be paid, provided the court is asked to deal with this before the end of the period specified.
(iii) *An order for maintenance for a specific term which cannot be extended.* This can only be changed in regard to the amount of money being paid. The court tends not to allow such orders to be made when, for example, there is a young family.
(iv) *An order dismissing maintenance immediately – the immediate 'clean break'.* This is only feasible if both parties are capable of being self-sufficient, or should be self-sufficient, both in the short and long term.

Linda and John were in their late thirties when they divorced. They had two children under five. Linda had had an administrative job before she stopped work to have the children, and was earning £15,000 per year. John worked for an insurance company and was earning £27,000 per annum.

While negotiating about their finances, they agreed that it would not be possible to have a clean break. The only capital they had was the equity in their home (in other words the value of the home less what is owed on the mortgage). The house was worth £80,000, and there was still £35,000 owing on the mortgage. Linda clearly needed maintenance in the short term, but what about the long term?

John argued that she would go back to work when the children were in full-time education. Linda felt uncertain about this, because she already felt out of date with office technology.

Linda also rejected John's suggestion that the maintenance for her be limited to a period of five years, which in his view would give her time enough to get back to work.

After taking advice from solicitors, they agreed that John should have a greater share of the capital from the home when it was ultimately sold, on the basis that Linda would have been receiving maintenance to herself on an open-ended basis. This also dealt with her concern about her long-term pension rights.

Five years on, after the original divorce and financial settlement, Linda's parents died and she was left £100,000. At that point John asked for her maintenance to come to an end, and her right to claim it in the future to be dismissed. Linda agreed that her future pension needs were now catered for, but she still felt insecure in the job market despite having worked on a part-time basis for two years. John agreed to continue to pay her maintenance for a fixed term of three years, which Linda in turn agreed could not be extended beyond that period.

NB: If the reverse had happened and John were the one who had inherited a large sum of money, then provided the Family Law Act 1996 were fully in force, Linda could have asked the court to award her a further capital sum for a clean break. Under the existing law (i.e. before the Family Law Act 1996 comes into force) John can volunteer to pay a further lump sum, which may or may not be enough for a clean break, but he cannot be forced to do so.

(3) Housing Needs

When considering the capital resources of the family, as distinct from the income resources, the central issue is usually the family home.

This is often the first issue to be dealt with, after short-term maintenance arrangements, because it governs the framework of the overall settlement.

One immediate concern is whether it is possible to keep the family home at all, when after separation there are likely to be two households with the same level of income to support them.

When the mortgage is large, this may mean that keeping the house is impossible.

The desire for continuity, especially where children are concerned, is a valid one and can become an emotive issue. Most couples try as hard as they can, for this reason, to keep the matrimonial home in one or the other's hands. There are many persuasive reasons for doing so. A mother of teenagers can passionately argue for minimising the disruption to their lives in the run-up to exams, for instance. Against this, their father may well argue that this would mean he cannot afford adequate housing himself where the children can visit and stay with him. Moreover, he might add that the resultant emotional fall-out from warring parents continuing to reside under the same roof would similarly disrupt the children.

In the face of this courts are generally anxious to ensure that if the bulk of capital from a house is being used to rehouse a mother (typically) and children, then the husband should not be deprived of all his capital. That is, the principle is that it is important that two households are established fairly. This is important above all so that children have somewhere to stay when they visit their father. As with maintenance, it is a difficult balancing exercise. Capital resources must be matched against the basic needs of both households.

One way in which it is possible to balance capital positions is to allow a proportion of the capital to be repaid later on. For example, where the bulk of the capital is used for rehousing a mother and children, it is possible for the father to be repaid a proportion of the capital when the children have left home. Very often this is expressed in terms of a 'legal charge' against the house.

This means that an appropriate amount is repayable, say, on the mother's remarrying or dying, or upon the youngest child reaching 18, depending upon which happens first. The housing needs of both the husband and the wife have to be anticipated for the medium- to long-term future. There may be adverse tax consequences of this formula, so these should be considered carefully with a solicitor.

For more affluent families it may be possible to sell other capital assets to raise money to purchase alternative properties.

Throughout the divorce process it is helpful to keep in mind the long-term needs of the family. In the rush to reduce emotional fall-out it is often tempting to agree on a quick financial settlement without sufficient regard to long-term consequences.

(4) Pensions and Life Assurance

One of the most difficult issues on divorce and separation concerns pensions. Despite recent changes in the law it is still difficult and in many cases impossible to achieve a fair solution. The legal problems are complex, as are their financial implications.

In most families, one spouse, usually the husband, will have been contributing to a pension scheme while the other, usually the wife, has not. By the time a couple are in their forties or fifties, the value of these pension funds can be considerable. Two questions arise. First, how can the value of a pension fund be dealt with fairly, when the family's assets are being sorted out? Secondly, how can a spouse who has no pension save up in time for his or her retirement, so that there is sufficient pension then?

It is not yet possible to split the capital value of pensions. In other words, if a husband has an occupational scheme through his employment (which may typically give him a percentage of his final salary when he retires), it is not possible for his wife to ask for part of the capital value of that pension to be transferred to her. New law is currently being prepared to enable pension-splitting to take place. However, this new law will not be available until roughly the year 2000.

One important new area of law, though, is already in force. The Pensions Act 1995 allows for 'earmarking' pensions. Provided no divorce or judicial separation proceedings were begun before 1st July 1996, it is possible to ask the Trustees to pay some or all of the benefits available under the pension scheme of one spouse to the other. For example, if a husband has an occupational pension through his job, it can be agreed that a share of his pension income will be paid to his wife, and so 'earmarked'. The position of the wife is more secure, because the Trustees of the pension scheme themselves are obliged to pay her.

Many pensions not only pay income but also lump sums on retirement. It is also possible to ensure that these lump sums are paid by the Trustees of the pension scheme to the other spouse. These are referred to in more detail below.

Importantly, courts now have a duty to consider pensions in every case. This is so even if retirement is many years off. Pensions will not be relevant in every single case; for example where the couple are in their twenties and in cases where the marriage has been a short one and there are no children.

The solutions which the Pensions Act has made available are similar to those already available. The solutions are maintenance or the payment of a lump sum as a means of providing support for a spouse who does not have a pension. The difference is that these payments can be relied on now even though they do not become effective for many years. The maintenance can be deferred for 20 or more years, until for example the husband has retired. The same is true of the lump sum payment, which a wife could use to supplement her own savings in providing an income for herself.

But there are practical problems. The husband may lose his job and with it will go the right to remain in that scheme and build up further savings with it. If the wife remarries she will lose the right to any maintenance, and this will include any part of the pension that had been set aside for her.

In more affluent families it is sometimes possible to reallocate other capital resources to help the spouse who has no pension to provide for the long-term future. For other families it may be necessary to consider maintenance orders on an open-ended basis. This would provide, for example, for the wife who has no pension, since her maintenance can be paid out of her husband's pension income. This will prevent the couple from having a clean break and being independent of each other financially, however.

One particular point to be borne in mind is the fact that on retirement many pensions provide a tax-free capital sum. With private pension policies this is usually about 25 per cent of their value. With occupational schemes it is sometimes possible to 'commute' part of the pension – in other words to take a lower income in return for a higher tax-free lump sum. The availability of this capital may form part of the solution if the couple are trying to achieve a clean break, since this lump sum can be given to the other spouse and invested to produce income.

It may well be that there is not enough capital available to provide an adequate income by the time retirement comes, even with a mixture of capital that is available now and capital that becomes available later. If so, the safest solution may be to keep maintenance rights open, and perhaps in addition to consider earmarking the income that will become available from any pension policy or pension scheme. Although this benefit will be lost if, for example, the wife who is to receive it remarries, it will provide an important safety net. It will always be possible to vary the maintenance which is available on retirement; if the amount of income is too low, it is possible to re-negotiate the sum that should be made available, and if it is not agreed then it is possible to ask the court to review it. This cuts both ways. If in this example the wife who was going to receive part of the pension income has herself received a major inheritance, then the husband may argue that she needs less of his pension income; he could then ask for the amount of maintenance which his pension scheme was to have paid to be reduced.

It is also important to consider what might happen if the person paying maintenance were to die. Is there enough life assurance in place to compensate the person receiving the maintenance? There is no point in negotiating a sum of maintenance to be paid to children or to a former spouse if the payer dies leaving them destitute.

It may not always be possible to afford life assurance but it should be considered. A cheaper alternative may be available if, for example, a husband has a contract of employment and receives a lump sum 'death in service'.

A word of warning about pensions: In every case, the terms the pension scheme or pension policy need to be looked at very carefully. The terms vary from scheme to scheme and policy to policy. The terms are complex and you are likely to need expert financial advice on these. You will also need the advice of a solicitor in helping you to structure the settlement when it comes to pensions. This is particularly the case if the further solution is to be considered, of varying the terms of a pension as if it were a trust or settlement. This is an additional solution to those set out above, one which has been developed through the courts rather than through new legislation from Parliament. This solution has more limited use because, for example, most occupational pension schemes are not susceptible to this type of application. Certain pensions are more susceptible to this type of approach, for example small self-administered schemes. There may be circumstances where such an application is helpful, because the benefits that it confers are not variable and would survive the remarriage of the person who benefits from the arrangement.

We have tried to set out some of the principles in dealing with pensions above. Hopefully, this has provided guidance as to what the overall objectives are when looking at this difficult area.

(5) What about His or Her New Partner?

In financial terms, the income and other financial resources of a new partner will only be relevant if the spouse is cohabiting with this new partner, or is likely to do so in the future. If so, the spouse has to disclose whatever information is known.

Similarly, if either spouse intends to remarry, this also has to be disclosed. This is particularly important if the spouse is or would have received maintenance. On remarriage, the right to receive maintenance comes to an end.

There is considerable scope for this area to become an emotional battleground. However, the resources of a new partner will only have an indirect bearing upon the overall negotiations. For example, if a wife is living with a new partner her husband may argue that he should no longer be paying full maintenance. If the partner is making a sufficient contribution towards the household this may be a valid argument.

Similarly, when a husband is living with a new partner his ex-wife may contend that he can and should afford to pay more maintenance to her if the new partner pays, or should pay, something towards his outgoings. As his expenses are relieved, the ex-wife can reasonably argue that more income is available for her and her children's requirements. However, it is not the case that his new partner will be required to contribute directly to maintenance.

In such circumstances where painful, jealous and hostile feelings can be aroused, restraint is recommended, if frequently in short supply. If children are involved, the new partner may have a vital role to be worked out eventually, in particular as a step-parent.

(6) Family Money: Inheritances

Another emotional battleground is money that has come from one or both spouses' families – or money that is likely to do so in the future.

The court approaches such matters as follows:

- If money has already been given to a spouse, then that money forms part of the resources which can be divided. The source of the money is relevant, and can be stated at the disclosure stage. But it is likely that the financial resources in their entirety, including gifts from parents, will be used in meeting the family's new needs.
- The courts will not usually place great reliance upon potential inheritances. They are often considered to be too remote, and may in any case be required for future use. Many elderly people get through a considerable amount of capital in meeting their nursing or other needs themselves. Also, potential provision under a will can be changed at any time and so cannot be guaranteed.

- Disclosure of *definite* inheritances is expected. For example, if one of the spouses' parents has died leaving the other a life interest in a property, it may be that the spouse has an interest now in the residuary estate which will be realised on the death of the surviving parent. If so, there is a duty to disclose this. This is so even if it may still be too remote to have any bearing on financial negotiations, perhaps because the other parent or step-parent is relatively young. Certainly if either spouse is the beneficiary of a trust already in existence, then full disclosure should be given of that intent.
- If the parents of one spouse or other has property in a different country then this may be directly relevant. In other jurisdictions, children have a strict right at law to inherit property and the property which is owned abroad will be governed by the law in that country. If that is the case, such property may be considered as a definite financial resource, but it will still be possible for that spouse's parents to sell the property and move the proceeds back to this country, or they may still be relatively young so that the prospect of their death will be considered too remote.

(E) The Child Support Agency

Another issue that will arise when parents separate is how the children's financial needs will be met.

There can be no clean break (dismissal of maintenance rights) between parents and children. Maintenance is usually paid for children until they reach the age of 17 or cease full-time secondary education, whichever is later, but may also cover further and higher education. The parents' responsibility to provide financially for their children has now been set down in the Child Support Act 1991, which came into force on 5th April 1993. The following relates to the situation where there has either been no agreement or court order relating to child maintenance prior to that date.

The Child Support Act governs the level of maintenance that should be paid by a biological parent who is not living with the parent who has primary care of the child. It does not cover step-children or school fees, but covers biological children up to the age of 17, or 19 if they are in certain types of full-time education, unless they have been adopted by another person. It does not cover higher education.

The Child Support Act sets out a formula to calculate the level of child maintenance payable by the 'absent parent'. This starts from what is known as the 'Maintenance Requirement', which is the amount deemed necessary to meet a child's needs, varying in accordance with the child's age. This formula is then used to work out what each parent can afford to pay, based upon their respective income and certain outgoings, including housing costs.

If parents are sharing care of the children, with the children spending at least 104 nights with the parent other than the primary carer, this shared-care situation will be reflected in the amount of maintenance assessed.

If the parent with primary care of the children is on Income Support, Family Credit or Disability Working Allowance, he or she is obliged by the Department of Social Security to apply for an assessment by the Child Support Agency, the organisation set up to assess, collect and enforce maintenance payments for children. If that parent refuses to make an application, he or she will be penalised by having benefit payments reduced. The only exception is where that parent can show that he or she, or any child living with him or her, would suffer undue harm or distress if the application was made and the other parent contacted. This might be where there is a history of violence.

Where the parent with primary care is not on such benefits, he or she may apply to the Agency for an assessment. However, such parents may prefer to try to agree a figure for child maintenance, bearing in mind the sort of amount that would be assessed under the Child Support Act. If divorcing, this figure can be embodied into a court order by agreement, which usually also deals with *all* of the financial aspects arising out of the divorce. If a figure cannot be agreed, the only option is for either parent to apply for an assessment through the Child Support Agency.

Given the inflexibility of the Agency's workings there are many advantages in seeking to agree child maintenance as part of an overall package.

If the parent with whom the child does not have primary residence is able to afford to make a further payment for child maintenance in addition to that calculated under the Child Support Act, a court may order that parent to make additional payments. A court can also make an order for school fees, maintenance for step-children or increased maintenance for disabled children and also for those in further and higher education, where the Child Support Act does not apply.

If a couple have a written agreement or court order prior to 5th April 1993, that remains in force until such time as the Child Support Agency intervenes. If either party receives the state benefits specified above, the parent with primary care may be obliged to apply to the Child Support Agency for an assessment, at which point that court order or agreement will cease to have effect. However, if that parent is not on benefits, the court will retain its jurisdiction indefinitely under current legislation. Therefore any variations for maintenance will be determined by the court, rather than by the Child Support Agency.

As with maintenance between spouses, maintenance payable for children through the courts can be changed if the parents' circumstances change. Similarly, if there has been a Child Support Act assessment, a re-assessment can either be made when the original is automatically reviewed (currently once every two years) or upon either parent's application when there is a change of circumstances.

Difficult though it can be for parents, children do benefit if matters relating to financial support for them are kept separate from discussions about their day-to-day care, emotional well-being and contact arrangements. These issues are discussed more fully in Section 4 and in Chapter 1.

6

THE EMOTIONAL ASPECTS OF SEPARATION

The point of separation is a crucial one in the divorce process. The family starts to live in two separate homes. Spouses are letting go, however slowly, of their attachment to each other as marital partners. The emphasis moves now to their shared role as parents. Adjustments may need to be made in coping with a host of new duties and routines concerning the children.

For most children the hardest stage emotionally is just after separation. Yet after separation there is often little co-operation between parents in supporting their children emotionally, because it is often the hardest time for parents as well. Moreover, just after separation is when hostility between them is frequently greatest. Whether displayed graphically or covertly, children are naturally upset.

As we have seen in Chapter 1, just after separation the bulk of the stress derives from loss and change. The more disruptions children experience in the process of divorce and its aftermath, the more trouble they seem to have.

Each family member undergoes his or her own mourning process over the loss, at the very least of the intact family. Sometimes the extent of the distress, with its accompanying hard feelings, prevents the couple from moving on. It can be difficult for a relationship to move to one of necessary co-operation if one or the other parent feels unwilling or unable to do so. It can also be difficult to support children's attachment to the other parent and to find energy to realign relationships and roles within the extended family and the community.

In short, how smoothly the process of separation proceeds for the couple and their children will depend on:

- the reasons for ending the marriage;
- the timing in the process for each partner;
- the emotional acceptance of the separation;
- the degree of agreement on legal and financial matters;
- the arrangements for the children;
- the involvement of third parties.

Children often feel that they are caught up in a drama in which they and their parents are out of phase. In addition, one spouse is usually ready to separate before the other. A parent may want children to move as fast or as slowly as he or she is moving. Children feel confused and anxious anyway, but especially if each parent is moving emotionally at a different rate through the separation phase.

If an impasse is reached and parents are stuck, if children are upset or disturbed as a result, counselling may be helpful. If parents are stuck on a specific problem, such as housing or contact arrangements, then mediation may help to come up with solutions or partial solutions.

Both from children's and parents' point of view the new family after separation differs from the former family in its composition and in the way it operates. Roles and rules change, and need to change, after separation. The pre-separation pattern of parenting – whether it is one of mutuality and co-operation or of conflict and non-co-operation, is replaced by the day-to-day responsibility of a single adult, in most cases the mother, who is the one with whom the children primarily reside.

When Mike and Lucy divorced they intended to carry on coparenting their four-year-old daughter, as they had done when married. While they were living together everything had been divided down the middle: bath nights alternated between the parents, and while one cooked dinner the other read or played with her. While one dressed her one morning, the other packed her bag for nursery. For their first six months apart the time was split down the middle again, only this time in different houses, dividing the week in half. But then Lucy met the man she eventually married. At first their arrangement suited the new romance, because it meant that Lucy was unencumbered for half the week. But as the relationship grew more serious this balance was threatened. What utterly changed matters was Lucy's fiancé's move to a different job in a different town and Lucy's decision to go with him. A battle over residence loomed, and then subsided, but the resolution meant that one residence would be the child's main one; the other parent would have to accept contact visits. For the past six years this primary residence has been with Lucy, although their daughter spends every weekend and almost all holidays with Mike. Coparenting has been practically impossible, although Mike tries to keep as abreast as possible about the child's life during his absence. The emotional bond between father and daughter is still very strong, but in fact Lucy simply knows more about the day-to-day facts and texture of their daughter's life than Mike.

(A) The Primary Carer

If a marriage has been deeply unsatisfactory, and especially if there has been violence, separation followed by single parenthood can be a relief and a positive challenge, despite financial hardships. In most cases, however, single parenthood is very difficult. Coping without practical and emotional support from the other parent can be overwhelming for some. The major points of hardship are:

- carrying the major burden for the children's welfare and schooling;
- fitting in time for or finding employment;
- discriminatory attitudes toward single parenting (especially toward mothers);
- social change, such as participating in social activities alone;
- emotional consequences, such as loneliness, coping with feelings about separation, anxiety about the future or jealousy if your spouse has a new partner or partners.

Most parents do adapt, as they learn strategies and skills for handling family life on their own. Most are helped immeasurably by practical and emotional support from other adults, such as relatives and friends, and by a civil and co-operative relationship with their ex-spouses. Establishing connections with other single parents, again for practical and emotional support as well as to normalise their own experiences, is probably the key to eventual good adjustment. There are often support groups – notably through churches and community centres – to enable this to happen.

Sue was 35 and living abroad when her husband Charlie announced that he was not going to return with the family when his job ended. Their marriage was turbulent — Charlie had hit her on numerous occasions and she had locked him out of the house a number of times after particularly vicious rows. Sue arranged to find another flat for her and their three children, in the foreign city in which they lived, and she carried on with the teaching job she had managed to secure. But she felt extremely lonely, exhausted and demoralised as she struggled to run this new house, in a new neighbourhood where she had few friends or distractions and while she tried to settle her three unruly and angry children into their new home and life without father. She slept badly, had difficulty helping the children with homework because her concentration and patience were short, and had little energy to keep the house organised or tidy.

After a year she decided to move back to the UK with the children to be near her family and friends. By then she and Charlie could speak civilly about arrangements. Charlie would visit monthly to see the children, and they would go out to him on holidays. Within six months Sue found that she could run things very smoothly, if very differently to the way she had under a shared roof with Charlie. The children went to bed an hour later so they could relax a bit more with her in the evenings; the dishes were not always done every night but there was always plenty to eat and lots of people dropping in.

Sue found she was less formal and much more comfortable, and her children were markedly more relaxed. Spending time with her family and friends, who would pitch in when she needed baby-sitting or help in fixing things around the house, and with whom she could spend a pleasant evening or afternoon just chatting, helped Sue ease into a new style of living which she found suited her and the children much better than her old one. She joined a singing group, which had as members a number of mainly single mothers like herself. These women made her feel normal. None of them had super-neat houses, all of them felt they were often running on empty, but most – especially those who had been divorced for longer than she – relished their independence and having control of their day-to-day lives.

(B) The Children

As we have said, the hardest stage for children during the whole process is usually just after separation. In Chapter 1 we stated a number of important things to bear in mind which children need especially at this time. These points will need repeating at the point of, and just after, separation.

It can be very difficult for children to understand what is happening. They need:

- constant explanations;
- updated information;
- emotional support, understanding and reassurance;
- an opportunity to talk about their feelings and worries.

Explanations of what is happening need to be tempered by what is reasonable to expect of the particular child given his or her personality, development and age. The most painful position for any child is that of being 'piggy in the middle', acting as messenger between embattled parents. It can be difficult to balance the encouragement of responsibility, which can help a child mature, with overloading the child with the adult responsibilities of the parent who has left.

(C) The Parent Who Does Not Live with the Children

The parent who usually lives apart from the children above all contends with the loss of daily intimacy with his or her children and with being out of touch with their routines. Coupled with this is the fear that the relationship will dissipate and even eventually disappear.

According to research, frequency of contact between a divorced father and his children appears to depend on social background, employment and income; the higher the income, the more the contact. This is probably in part because such parents more easily can afford travel and entertainment expenses incurred because of contact arrangements with children, and may have more job flexibility to enable it. A stunning research finding is that 50 per cent of divorced fathers who do not live with their children lose contact within two years of the divorce.

Behind these findings lies the implication that to ensure continuation of their relationship, parents need to commit time, money, energy and patience. Those parents who do so normally not only remain in relationships with their children but also can find them improved. Other studies have shown that the quality of the relationship post-separation and divorce is not contingent on the quality of the relationship beforehand. Fathers who have had formerly distant or conflictual relationships with their sons, for instance, or mothers with difficult relationships with their daughters or, on the other hand, parents who had been close and loving with their children before divorce, all may find their relationships utterly different afterwards. Indeed, some parents who had been close before even lose contact. This is because so many other variables can intervene. These include the amount of co-operation between parents in enabling contact; the forbearance needed to overcome children's resentment; the children's and your own pain on partings and reunions; whether new partners, among others, encourage relationships with children post-divorce; as well as how much time and energy is and can be invested.

David built up his own highly successful property development company. He and Vicky married in their early twenties and went on to have three children. He says that they married because Vicky became pregnant and he felt railroaded into marriage. As soon as the children came, the gulf between them, already apparent within months of their wedding, grew larger. They rowed constantly and David stayed away from home, working more and more. He saw his children on Sunday mornings, when he took them swimming, and occasionally in the evening just as they would be going to bed. Mornings he left before anyone else arose, and Saturdays were spent working. He regretted how little time he spent with his children, but more than that he wanted to avoid their mother. The couple finally separated when Vicky met someone else and insisted that David move out. Incensed at the loss of control over his life which he now faced, David insisted on frequent contact with the children. He now found himself delegating jobs at work so that he could be free each Wednesday evening, when he had the children, and all day Sunday, and every other Saturday. He discovered that he enjoyed his children, found them interesting to observe and talk to; he started tennis lessons together with them and eventually they found a shared interest in the sport. Certainly for David divorce spelled a better and richer relationship with his children than his loveless and difficult marriage had done.

The parent who lives apart also must contend with other losses and changes in routine and resources. A discussion of these appears in Chapter 1.

(D) New Partners

Most people eventually become involved with new partners. Sometimes this happens before the separation, making the marital breakdown more complicated. This is for two main reasons. First it is because the wife or husband must deal with the extremely painful effects of a spouse's affair in addition to marital breakdown. Second it is because children are often quite unreasonably expected immediately to take on a relationship with someone they will normally view as an enemy of the other parent, and this at the same time they are taking in what is for them the terrible fact of their family's breakdown.

Sometimes new partners enter the scene after a couple have separated or divorced. It should be noted here that this may happen in addition to what is described above, because many affairs do not in the end lead to marriage. Children may have to encounter a number of new partners in their divorced parents' lives. Each new partner poses a new dilemma for the children, as well as for the ex-spouses. How seriously do we take this relationship? Will it last or break down as the last did? Is it worth investing energy and faith into making a relationship with this person work, or will it end, leaving me depleted, confused and neglected again? Children ask these questions, just as their parents do. New partners disrupt the status quo of routines, habits and expectations. They take a good deal of energy and commitment on the part of children to adjust to. They also threaten past loyalties between children and their parents. Children can understandably feel jealous of a new person claiming their mother's or father's time and attention, especially if they are also understandably wary about this person's staying or taking a sincere interest in them.

Occasionally there are particularly difficult situations involving new partners, such as .when there have been prior sorts of relationships with them (such as when the new partner is the parent of one of your children's friends, or your ex-spouse's new partner is your own best friend) or when the new partnership is homosexual. These are situations which have unusual properties and require more patient expectations of your children's adjustment. They may also require professional advice or help, or counselling for both parents and children. In the case of prior existing relationships, children most often will feel confused and quite often betrayed; they had thought they understood that certain boundaries were not to be crossed. In the case of homosexual liaisons children also feel confused and, because society does not universally support such unions, they also at first may feel ashamed.

These cases are complicated usually by lack of support from the wider community as well. Friends, relatives and neighbours may frown on the new liaisons and take sides. Children are often left with little support or help about how to come to terms with their parents' new relationships. Yet without such support they may not accept them.

Their non-acceptance of any new romantic liaison can be fatal – either to the parent's new relationship or to their relationship with that parent. This lack of support, as well as everyone's understandable bewilderment, coupled with their own strong feelings may call for professional assistance. Such help can intervene, with guidance, before any of the various relationships becomes damaged.

section 3

LEGAL PROCEEDINGS IN DIVORCE

7

DIVORCE PROCEEDINGS

The law of divorce is inadequate in its present form. Anyone contemplating ending a marriage should be alive to the potential pitfalls and may wish to address with his or her solicitor how best to minimise the impact of the existing legislation on the family. In this part of the book we shall be illustrating the shortcomings of the legal framework to help you do the same with your solicitor.

Until the new law of divorce is introduced (in 1998 or 1999) the procedure for obtaining a divorce in England and Wales remains as described below. What follows is a summary of the law relating to divorce as it stands, highlighting where problems can arise and how best to deal with them.

Contrary to popular belief, there is only one ground for divorce: that the marriage has irretrievably broken down. However, the court cannot hold that a marriage has broken down irretrievably until the petitioner (that is, whoever initiates the divorce proceedings) proves one or more of the following five facts as specified in the Matrimonial Causes Act 1973 – namely:

1. adultery – the respondent (the other spouse) has committed adultery and the petitioner finds it intolerable to live with the respondent;

2. unreasonable behaviour – the respondent has behaved in such a way that the petitioner cannot reasonably be expected to live with the respondent;
3. desertion – the respondent has deserted the petitioner for a continuous period of two years;
4. two years' separation – the parties have lived apart for a continuous period of two years and the respondent consents to a divorce;
5. five years' separation – the parties have lived apart for five years.

Details of the fact or facts being relied upon are presented to the court in the 'petition', which is the document filed at court to commence the divorce proceedings.

It is indicative of how nonsensical the existing law is that the petitioner does not have to prove that the facts upon which his or her petition are based are those which actually led to the breakdown of the marriage. For example, it is quite possible for one spouse to obtain a divorce against the other based on the latter's adultery, even when that adultery only took place after the couple had separated.

This kind of anomaly can create tensions even between couples who agree as a matter of principle that they wish to separate. Understandably, neither party to a marriage wishes to be made out to be the 'bad guy', but the present system is such that approximately 75 per cent of divorces in England and Wales proceed on 'fault-based' petitions (i.e. adultery or unreasonable behaviour). One of the reasons behind these statistics is that unless a husband and wife are prepared to wait for a period of separation of two years or more to elapse, they have no alternative other than to file a fault-based petition to commence divorce proceedings. Often, particularly in the case of brief marriages or where the parties are young and there are no children, they wish to sever their ties and move forward in their lives as quickly as possible.

In practice, many couples agree that they just want to get on with their divorce. Often there will have been no adultery, in which case the only expedient option is to allege unreasonable behaviour (desertion being very rarely relied upon). The irony is that during the breakdown of a marriage, both parties will inevitably have behaved 'unreasonably' at some stage: the spouse who is ultimately petitioned against may understandably feel affronted that the petition tells only one side of what is often a complex story. Sometimes, the knee-jerk response is to retaliate and for the respondent to want to put his or her side of the story and so defend the proceedings.

The examples described above are all tensions created by the existing system. The new law advocates a non-adversarial approach in which many of these problems do not arise, not least because the five facts proving irretrievable breakdown will be dispensed with.

If you are reading this book with a view to initiating divorce proceedings, whether unilaterally or in agreement with your spouse, it is hoped that you will gain an awareness of how the system itself might impose on your situation. You will then be armed with some ideas on how to manage the process, with a view to minimising the scope for bitterness and conflict and so promote a conciliatory approach.

When both of you want to proceed with divorce, it is possible to agree who will be the petitioner and on what fact the divorce petition will be based. A solicitor may then suggest sending the 'respondent' a draft of the divorce petition before it is filed at the court, so that anything which may cause particular offence can be reconsidered. There may be some instances where this approach is not appropriate. For most couples, though, this is the least contentious way of getting the divorce up and running. Couples in this situation often agree to split the costs of the divorce suit and the court fees equally between them. Essentially, therefore, the decision to divorce becomes a joint one. Psychologically, each of you can feel that the proceedings are within your control.

In many cases, however, the decision to divorce will not be a joint one. Often, one spouse will want to end a marriage quickly, perhaps to embark on a new life with a new partner. Whoever is on the receiving end of such a decision finds him or herself not only having to cope emotionally and on a practical level with the impact of separation, but may even be placed in the invidious position of being pushed into initiating divorce proceedings which he or she does not want. Sometimes enormous pressures will be brought to bear on the spouse who does not wish to divorce, to file a petition based on the other's adultery, or otherwise risk having an 'unreasonable behaviour' petition filed against him or her. Solicitors rarely advise clients to defend a divorce petition, as there is little to be gained in doing so if the marriage is at an end and the legal costs are prohibitive and often difficult to justify. This feeling of being 'bulldozed', added to the other emotions which come into play (*see Chapter 1*) creates a profound sense of injustice which then inevitably has an impact on the injured spouse's attitude towards other negotiations relating to finances and the children.

At the opposite end of the spectrum, the feelings of guilt experienced by the spouse leaving the marriage can mean that he or she feels disempowered from initiating divorce proceedings. He or she would rather the other relieved him or her of that responsibility. This can often distort the spouses' respective bargaining positions in relation to wider issues such as finances or arrangements for the children. For example, a wife may refuse to file divorce proceedings until financial matters have been settled. In this situation a husband may find himself conceding more than he might otherwise be expected to, in order to secure his wife's co-operation in the divorce or, worse still, arrangements for contact with the children.

We have suggested in Chapter 4 that there may be advantages in postponing issuing divorce proceedings so that more immediate concerns relating to the children and finances can be addressed in isolation.

Our advice to those contemplating divorce is that they should approach issuing divorce proceedings in the least contentious way possible by agreeing as much as possible beforehand. This will avoid the need for either spouse to seek to achieve psychological one-upmanship, and should minimise the impact of the shortcomings in the law upon other legal and practical issues.

Turning then to the practicalities, how are divorce proceedings begun and how can you adopt a conciliatory approach?

(A) The Divorce Petition

On page 96 is a flow chart setting out the basic procedure for divorce. The first step is for the petitioner to file the divorce petition at the court. The contents of the petition are prescribed by the Family Proceedings Rules 1991. The petition is made up of basic information about the parties to the marriage, the date and place of the marriage, and any children in the family.

The petition must contain a statement that the petitioner considers the marriage to have broken down irretrievably, and the petitioner must then recite one of the five 'facts' described above and give particulars to support this statement of fact. It is the impact of these particulars which can often cause unnecessary ill-feeling if care is not taken. Allegations which are inflammatory and unnecessary in proving the fact are best avoided. (Ways of presenting the information required in the petition are considered later.)

The petition contains a request for the court to dissolve the marriage. For technical reasons, the petition also asks the court to consider the financial claims, and it does this even if all these aspects have already been agreed. It is also usual for the petitioner to require the respondent, within the petition itself, to pay the legal costs of the divorce. If the couple are approaching the divorce in a co-operative way, it will help to discuss who pays for the divorce beforehand. For example, the couple may agree to share the costs and to state this in the petition.

The petition, together with the Marriage Certificate, a court fee (currently £150) and a Statement of Arrangements for Children (where there are any) is filed at the court. The petitioner's solicitor is also required to file a certificate stating whether or not the solicitor has discussed with the petitioner the possibility of a reconciliation and given him or her details of agencies qualified to help where this is a possibility.

There is no duty on a solicitor to explore with a client whether the marriage has broken down irretrievably. We suggest that a good solicitor should offer information about local counselling agencies or private practitioners, such as marital or family therapists, and to discuss whether there is any possibility of a reconciliation with you. Even if you are faced with a *fait accompli* because your spouse has indicated that there is no possibility of a reconciliation, your solicitor can recommend various sources of help to assist you and your children in coming to terms with the decision to separate.

How then can you, as the petitioner, ensure that your petition is drafted in the least contentious way possible? The bulk of the information contained in the petition is prescribed by law and is factual. The particulars of the petition are, however, at the petitioner's discretion and you should always ensure that you see what is put in the particulars of the petition. Most solicitors will ask you to approve draft particulars in any event. It is worth, therefore, at this juncture, itemising the facts upon which a petition can be based, and highlighting particular aspects which you may wish to consider.

(1) Adultery

It is no longer a requirement to name the co-respondent (i.e. the person with whom the respondent has committed adultery). The petitioner can simply state that the identity of the person with whom the respondent has committed adultery is known to him or her, but that he or she does not wish to name that person.

It is now regarded as a 'hostile' stance if the petitioner names the co-respondent. There is no legal benefit in doing so (except occasionally on the issue of costs). However aggrieved the petitioning spouse may be feeling towards the third party there is little to be gained by including third parties in divorce proceedings.

Although it will not always be the case, adultery is often symptomatic of a marriage which is in difficulty, as opposed to being the root cause of the difficulties. A great number of spouses whose partners have had affairs are understandably reluctant to accept this to be the case and often see the divorce petition as an opportunity both to absolve themselves from any blame for the breakdown of the marriage and also as an opportunity publicly to expose the other spouse and humiliate the co-respondent.

Someone who is issuing a petition based on his or her spouse's adultery is likely to feel badly let down, deceived and humiliated. But using the petition as a device to get one's own back may only be cathartic in the short term. Naming a co-respondent, given the lack of necessity to do so, is likely to be viewed as adversarial and may lead to further polarisation between you and your spouse extending beyond the divorce suit itself to far more important issues such as the children and finances.

(2) Unreasonable Behaviour

Petitions based on 'unreasonable behaviour' offer the most scope for causing unnecessary offence.

A petition based on this fact must contain a number of allegations and specific examples of the type of unreasonable behaviour complained of. No objective test is applied by the court as to whether the average person would consider the alleged behaviour to be unreasonable. The test is subjective in that only the petitioner must find it so.

For every unreasonable behaviour petition filed, it is worth bearing in mind that the respondent to that petition could probably file a cross-petition based on the petitioner's unreasonable behaviour.

There are of course varying degrees of unreasonable behaviour and we do not seek to trivialise the pain associated with this. We of course acknowledge that there are always going to be cases where it simply will not be appropriate to advocate a conciliatory or joint approach to issuing divorce proceedings. For example, this is the case where there has been violence and abuse. But in the main, if allegations of unreasonable behaviour can be expressed in such a way that they will not provoke the person on the receiving end to feel compelled to defend them, so much the better. The benefit of keeping conflict and retaliation to a minimum at this point is incalculable.

A defended divorce means increased animosity; it also runs up costs. It is not unusual for a respondent to an unreasonable behaviour petition to file an answer, stating that he or she intends to defend the petition, only for the respondent later to accept that there is little point in doing so, not least from a cost point of view. The ill-feeling aroused in the respondent by having to 'step down' will inevitably spill over into other discussions; in most cases this situation is therefore best avoided in the first place.

(3) Desertion, Two- and Five-Years' Separation

The particulars of these three facts are usually fairly uncontentious insofar as they recite matters of fact, as opposed to matters of opinion. It is however worth ensuring that anything which is likely to be contentious (such as the date upon which the parties are deemed to have separated) is accurate and has been agreed.

It is not uncommon for one spouse to want to make the other wait as long as possible for the divorce to be finalised, particularly when there have been periods of separating and trial reconciliation prior to the final separation. Careful attention needs to be paid to when the period of separation can really be said to have begun. It is worth noting that spouses can live 'separate and apart' under the same roof in particular circumstances, and such time can be included in the calculation of the two or five years.

Where a petition is based on a two-year or five-year separation, there is a legal mechanism by which the respondent can prevent the Decree Nisi being made into a Decree Absolute, which is the point at which the marriage is finally dissolved. It is also possible to defend a petition based on five-years' separation if there would be grave financial or other hardship. (The new legislation proposes to extend this defence to all forms of divorce.)

Moving on from the petition, what other documents are filed at the court when divorce proceedings are issued?

In Chapter 9 we refer to the Solicitors Family Law Association Code of Practice. The code recommends that solicitors should consider, with their clients, contacting the other party or his or her solicitor in advance as to the intention of filing a petition and the 'fact' on which the petition is to be based.

(B) Statement of Arrangements for Children

This is a standard form which gives details about the children in the family. It provides the court with the information it needs in order to consider arrangements for them. The form covers accommodation, education, child-care, health, child maintenance and arrangements which have been made or which are proposed for contact with the parent with whom the child is not going to live full-time. If the child is disabled or has any medical problems then the form may be supported by a medical report or doctor's letter, giving details of the problem and its likely effect on the child. The petitioner must always sign this form personally.

Wherever practicable, the contents of the form should be agreed with the respondent parent, who should also sign it so that it can be submitted to the court jointly. If there is disagreement between the parties on any aspect of arrangements for the welfare of the children it is open to the respondent parent to file his or her own separate Statement of Arrangements for Children.

This form now encourages both parents to recognise and support the continuing parental role of the spouse with whom the children do not live. The new approach emphasises that both parents need to recognise their joint responsibility to work together in the best interests of their children regardless of the breakdown of their relationship. No one underestimates how difficult this can be when emotional temperatures are running high and negative feelings prevail between the spouses.

However, the fact remains that children will do best if their parents can agree and are seen to be agreeing over arrangements for them. This is particularly so regarding their contact with the parent with whom they are not going to live. We have advocated that these issues ought to be discussed well in advance of any final decision being made about the marriage in any event. Nonetheless, the risk of conflict relating to the children later on ought to be minimised if the parents try to agree on the Statement of Arrangements, at least. It is important to word the Statement of Arrangements neutrally and that it is not seen as an attempt by the primary carer to dictate what he or she will 'allow' the other parent in relation to the children.

There is a more detailed description of the law relating to children in Section 5.

Once the divorce petition and supporting documentation have been filed at the court, they must be served on the respondent. When the respondent has already seen a solicitor, that solicitor is likely to be instructed to 'accept service' of the petition on behalf of the respondent. This means the documentation is sent to the solicitor, rather than to the respondent directly.

Although the law allows the petitioner simply to ask the court to post the petition to the respondent at his or her home, the upset that this can cause, particularly if the respondent has no idea that divorce proceedings have been issued, is something which should be avoided.

Very occasionally there will be good reasons why a petition should be served on the respondent personally, rather than sent to his or her solicitor. This will involve a 'process server' attending the respondent in person and serving the documents on him or her. Inevitably, this is likely to be at the respondent's home or even at his or her place of work, and will only be necessary, or in our view justifiable, in exceptional circumstances. For example, if it is known that the respondent will try to evade service of the petition or when previous attempts to serve the documents have failed, serving in this way may be necessary.

Once served with divorce proceedings, the respondent must file an Acknowledgement of Service at the court. This is the respondent's opportunity to state whether he or she intends to defend the petition. When the petition is based on adultery the respondent has to say whether or not the alleged adultery is admitted. In the case of a period of two-years' separation, the respondent must say whether or not he or she consents to a decree being granted. The respondent must at this stage also state whether or not he or she agrees with the arrangements for children as set out in the Statement of Arrangements filed at the court. The respondent is invited to file his or her own Statement if there are issues relating to the children with which he or she does not agree.

Once the petitioner has proof that the respondent has been served with divorce proceedings, he or she can ask the court to dissolve the marriage. An Affidavit in Support of the Petition is filed; this is to confirm to the court that the contents of the petition are true. The petitioner also has to request that the divorce be listed for Decree Nisi. The District Judge then decides whether the matters alleged in the petition have been proved. If they have, the judge will grant a certificate that the matter should be placed in the 'special procedure' list. He or she will also, at this stage, certify whether the arrangements made for the children are satisfactory.

Prior to the implementation of the Children Act, divorcing couples were required to appear before a judge and explain the arrangements which had been put in place for the upbringing of the children. The judge had to be satisfied that the arrangements for the children were settled, that the frequency of contact between children and the parent with whom they were not living was adequate, and that adequate arrangements for child maintenance were in place. Only when these issues had been satisfactorily determined would the court allow the Decree Nisi to be pronounced.

One of the fundamental principles introduced by the Children Act was that of 'non-intervention'. It was felt generally that the parents, not the court, are best placed to decide what is right for their children. Under the new system, therefore, unless it is clear from the documents filed at the court by the respective parents that there is a dispute relating to parenting, the court will not seek to impose its views uninvited. (The mechanisms for applying to the court in cases where there is a dispute relating to the exercise of parental responsibility are referred to in Chapter 12.)

Assuming then that arrangements for children have been certified satisfactory, the court will then automatically list the matter for the pronouncement of the Decree Nisi and the parties will be notified of the date upon which it will be pronounced. The time it takes to obtain a date for the pronouncement of the Decree Nisi depends on the workload of the court. A two- to three-month wait from the date of filing the Affidavit in Support of Petition is not uncommon. The pronouncement of Decree Nisi is, in most cases, a formality. The District Judge reads out a list of people applying for Decree Nisi. There is no need for either of the parties or their solicitors to attend unless there is a dispute about who should pay the costs of the divorce suit.

Once the Decree Nisi has been pronounced, after six weeks and one day the petitioner can apply for the Decree Absolute. It is not until the granting of Decree Absolute that the marriage is dissolved.

At present, and also under the new law, it is not possible to present a petition for divorce within one year of marriage. Couples wishing to separate within this timescale can regulate their financial affairs in a Deed of Separation (*see Chapter 4*).

(C) The Timing of Finalising the Decree of Divorce

As will be seen from the flow chart on page 96, obtaining a decree of divorce is a two-stage process. There may be good reasons for ensuring that the decree of divorce is not finalised until financial matters have been sorted out. For example, for pension purposes a wife will lose her status as her husband's widow (and vice-versa) upon divorce. There may be similar implications for life assurance policies and other work-related benefits. Particularly in cases in which the husband has always been the principal wage-earner, he should not underestimate the vulnerability his wife will feel when she is no longer entitled to such benefits or a widow's pension. Care must be taken to ensure that appropriate, fair financial adjustments are made prior to granting of the final decree.

Inevitably, in some situations one party will be keener to have a divorce finalised than the other. Because in certain circumstances it is possible to delay the Decree Absolute until financial matters have been finalised, it is not uncommon for one party to use the Decree Absolute as a beating stick to obtain a more favourable financial deal. Clearly, using the timing of a decree as a bargaining tool will heighten tension. It is likely that if this happens it reflects an imbalance in bargaining powers.

(D) The New Law of Divorce

In place of the existing law, which we have gone into in some detail, the Government has introduced a much simpler legal framework. This new framework is intended to reduce the conflict between spouses and also to help save marriages which have not broken down beyond repair. This law will probably not come into force until late 1998 or 1999. Until then the existing law described above applies.

The main features of the new law are set out below.

(1) Information Sessions

There are some exceptions to this, but the vast majority of people will have to go through this process.

The nature of these information sessions are going to form part of a pilot scheme beginning in June 1997 and running until the early summer of 1998. The Government has committed itself to ensuring that the information sessions will be available on a

The Current Divorce Procedure

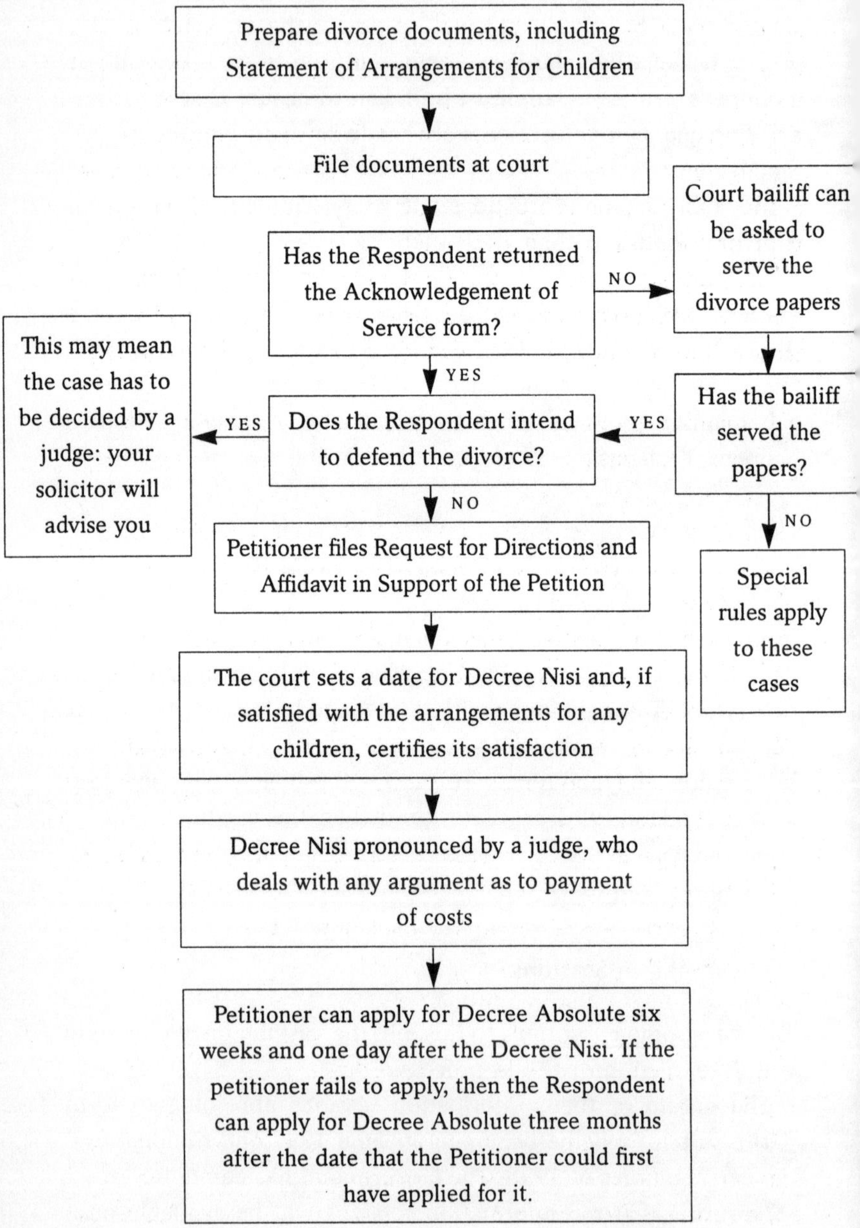

one-to-one basis. In other words, the information provider – someone who will be specifically appointed for this purpose – will have a meeting with whichever spouse wants to start off the process of divorce or separation through the courts. In addition there may also be group sessions, when information about the divorce process will be conveyed while other people contemplating divorce are also present. These group sessions have been successful in Australia, and the pilot scheme is being directed to see whether they will be helpful here.

The purpose of the information sessions is to ensure that those embarking on divorce realise the seriousness of the steps they are taking. Information will also be made available on the following:

- marriage counselling and other marriage support services;
- the importance to be attached to the welfare, wishes and feelings of children;
- how the parties may acquire a better understanding of the ways in which children can be helped to cope with the breakdown of a marriage;
- the nature of the financial questions that may arise on divorce or separation, and services which are available to help the parties;
- protection available against violence and how to obtain support and assistance;
- mediation;
- the availability to each of the parties of independent legal advice;
- the principles of Legal Aid and where the parties can get advice about obtaining Legal Aid;
- the divorce and separation process.

An information pack will be available at the meeting; videos may also be available.

Individual advice is *not* going to be available at the information session. It will still be necessary to see an independent solicitor to review issues affecting you as an individual in your case. However, a lot of free information will be available about mediation and about the legal process.

One of the main objects of the new law is to try and save marriages which are savable. The information session will concentrate on the marriage in question, to see if counselling or therapy has been considered in an effort to save it.

As well as the person who wants to file a Statement of Marital Breakdown (*see below*), the other spouse will have to attend an information session if he or she wishes:

- to apply for an order with respect to a child of the family;
- to apply for an order relating to property or financial matters; or
- to oppose an application for a divorce or a separation order.

The precise form of the information sessions will only be known after the pilot scheme has come to an end. At that point new legislation will set out the details more clearly.

(2) Statement of Marital Breakdown

The new law states that a party making a Statement of Marital Breakdown must have attended an information session not less than three months before making the Statement. Again, the precise workings of this will not be known until additional legislation has been drafted.

The process of divorce will then be started by one spouse, or the spouses jointly, filing a Statement of Marital Breakdown. The great advantage of the new law is that this will be a neutral document. There will not have to be any evidence of adultery or unreasonable behaviour or the other facts considered in this chapter. Much of the difficulty and unpleasantness can therefore be avoided. Most importantly, the prospects of saving the marriage will not be jeopardised by the legal process in the ways we have looked at above.

The Statement will have to be in a prescribed form. Additional rules will be created after the pilot scheme, setting out the details of the form. At this stage, we know that a statement has to be given that the marriage has broken down. It does not have to state that the marriage has broken down *irretrievably*. That will only be determined at the end of the period for reflection and consideration.

At this stage it will not be necessary to state whether the court is being asked to make a divorce or separation order. That question can wait until after the period of reflection and consideration.

(3) Period of Reflection and Consideration

At the very heart of the new law is the period of reflection and consideration. This begins 14 days after the Statement of Marital Breakdown has been filed at the court. It will only be possible to apply for a divorce or separation order after the ending of this period.

While this period goes on, it is hoped that the parties will reflect on the consequences of the marriage breaking down and consider saving the marriage. It is also hoped that all the necessary arrangements for the future about money and about children will be resolved during this period.

While the law went through Parliament there was much debate as to the length of the period of reflection and consideration. The final result of this debate is that the overall period from the date of the information session(s) to the date of the divorce order must not be less than one year.

The precise formula is more complicated. The period for reflection and consideration is nine months beginning with the 14th day after the Statement of Marital Breakdown is received by the court. As we have seen, this date must not be less than three months after the information session. During the 14-day period after the Statement of Marital Breakdown has been filed at the court, the other spouse is expected to be served with the

Statement. The effect of all of this is that the minimum period from the information session is therefore 54 weeks.

This period can be extended in certain circumstances, for example if there is a possibility of reconciliation. It is also possible for the other spouse, the non-initiating party, to apply for a delay of six months. The ability to delay the making of the divorce order once it has been applied for appears to be at the complete discretion of the non-initiating spouse. This is something that he or she may or may not wish to do, and it will not be questioned by the court.

The period for reflection and consideration must in any event be extended from nine months to 15 months where there is a child under 16 years old at the date of the application for the divorce order. This extension can only be prevented if the delay is shown to the court to be detrimental to the welfare of the child.

If a couple are already living apart before the new law is brought into force, it may be possible for this prior period of separation to be used within the divorce proceedings. As yet the regulations have not been drafted so the precise mechanics are not known. However, it is possible to envisage difficulties arising in the future where a couple have been living apart but cannot prove the fact. This is going to be particularly difficult for those who are living apart whilst remaining under the same roof. It may well be worth taking legal advice on this point if you are intending to use a period of living apart prior to the time when the new law comes into force.

It will not be possible in the majority of cases to obtain a divorce order unless the arrangements for the future are satisfied, either by producing a court order or a negotiated agreement regarding the finances. Alternatively it is possible to satisfy the court regarding financial arrangements by making a declaration that there are 'no significant assets' and that neither party intends to apply for financial provision, so that there are no arrangements to be made.

The new law also requires the court to be satisfied with the arrangements for the children of the family. The divorce order cannot be made until the judge has considered the arrangements which have been made or are proposed for the upbringing and welfare of the children, and can resolve whether or not to exercise any of the court's powers with respect to any of them. These provisions are similar to those described above in relation to the existing law. The new law places greater emphasis on the court considering the child's own wishes.

Although the intention of the new Act is to simplify the procedures, it can be seen that there is still scope for one or other party to delay the proceedings, perhaps for advantage in discussions about finances or the children. The scope is much less wide than under the existing legislation, but it remains nonetheless.

It is also possible to block a divorce if there is going to be substantial financial or other hardship to the other party or a child of the family. The person trying to block the divorce also has to show that it would be wrong in all circumstances for the marriage to be dissolved. This is similar to the existing 'hardship bar' which is available under the existing law in much more restricted circumstances. It remains to be seen the extent to which the courts will allow divorce orders to be blocked in this way. Again, there is more scope for tactical applications being made.

On balance, though, there are clear advantages to the new legislation. By avoiding having to give details of adultery or unreasonable behaviour, and all the contentious evidence which this entails, the new law is a major step forward for helping families while they are going through the trauma of marriage breakdown.

8

MEDIATION

The new law contained in the Family Law Act 1996 puts an emphasis on using mediation as a tool for limiting the damage in the divorce process. This is because, in theory, mediation assumes that the spouses are trying to work toward a common goal to achieve a divorce agreement that will be and feel as fair as possible to both and will also put any children's interests first and foremost. The traditional format for sorting out issues in divorce has been either negotiation between the spouses themselves – often through their solicitors – or resolving the issues through the courts. This traditional format does not explicitly promote either joint interests or the children's interests over the interests of each partner alone. It can, instead, very easily become adversarial, although very often of course it does not and can be irreproachably fair and sensible.

Over recent years, the third format for negotiation, mediation, has emerged. Rather than trying to deal with potentially heated matters directly or by employing solicitors to negotiate with each other, increasingly many couples are turning to mediation.

Mediation does not exclude using a solicitor. Solicitors can be consulted before, during and after a mediation agreement is reached. It is recommended to both parties to see a solicitor for independent advice about what has been discussed during the course of and after mediation has ended.

It is often not possible to deal with all issues in mediation, and a solicitor may have to be instructed about negotiating these directly. This need not imply that the mediation has failed, for it is likely that the way has been paved for an eventual agreement. The fact that the couple have attempted to discuss matters is in itself important.

(A) What Is Mediation for?

The purpose of mediation is to provide a setting in which divorcing couples can try to resolve matters, usually about finances, housing and their children's welfare, with the help of trained mediators. They help to manage discussions by acting as informed referees, ensuring that both points of view are dealt with fairly. With their help, the divorcing couple put on the agenda the matters they need to discuss. The mediators then manage these discussions.

However, there is one topic *not* appropriate for mediation: whether the marriage can still work or not – whether the relationship has broken down beyond repair. Mediation assumes that this is the case. Its purpose is to enable a couple to sort out issues arising out of separation or divorce and to help the couple focus on their and their children's future.

Because of the way it has evolved, many people now know that mediation can help with issues concerning children. For example, mediation can help couples arrive at a plan for children's contact with the parent who does not live with them. It can also be used to resolve children's residence (for example whether they live full-time with one parent, or part-time with both). Very commonly, mediation is used to sort out the contact arrangements – the times and other arrangements for the children to see the parent with whom they are not living. (The legal framework for residence and contact is dealt with in Chapter 12.) Mediation can also sort out how, when and under what conditions to allow the introduction to children of either parent's new partner.

In addition to child-care issues it is now also possible to take financial issues to mediation. The sort of financial issues that it deals with include maintenance payments; disposal of the family's capital (usually the home); pension arrangements and inheritances; interim arrangements for payment of jointly incurred expenses; and plans for payment of future joint expenses, such as children's future educational needs.

Mediation often begins by focusing on immediate concerns, such as children's welfare, housing and financial arrangements. Sometimes these are first settled for the interim, then more permanently. People can use mediation at any stage in the divorce process.

With financial issues mediation frequently needs to start with basic fact-finding, such as how much are the electricity, gas and water bills; how much is the house worth; what about savings, building society and bank accounts; how much will alternative housing cost? In this respect, at least, mediation helps cut costs, for the process of fact-finding is something which involves solicitors in much time and expense, but usually does not require legal expertise to be done successfully. In other words, basic fact-finding through the use of solicitors is a much more expensive option than doing so through mediation.

Mediation should enable each party to voice the anxieties and concerns to the other face-to-face. While that may seem daunting, it should be a help in reducing any misunderstandings.

(B) How Does Mediation Work?

The couple arrange to have a preliminary mediation session at which its aims are explained, and the couple set an initial agenda. Many, but not all, mediation cases are concluded within four to six sessions. This will of course largely depend upon the issues to be resolved.

Each person may be asked to consider before the next session alternatives to any present arrangements. They are usually asked to prepare a schedule of their expenditures and their assets. This information is then fed back into the mediation process at subsequent sessions, so that the couple can consider what practical options are available to them.

(C) The Role of Solicitors in Mediation

Mediation does not eliminate the need for your own solicitor. Before embarking on it many people do have at least an initial consultation with a solicitor. No solicitor can act for both people involved, and any solicitor acting as a mediator cannot act for either one spouse or the other.

Having independent advice at this stage is helpful for a number of reasons. Most importantly, it can enable you to set out clearly your own particular agenda and needs. It can also give you an expert perspective for your side of things. Your own solicitor is able to act as your consultant at all stages of mediation. For instance, once financial evidence has been gathered and disclosed your legal adviser can help you to consider this. This gives each party the opportunity to ensure all necessary financial information has been provided and to consider its relevance. Your solicitor may spot areas missing, giving suggestions about what additional information you may need and how you might obtain it.

Although the information gathered together in mediation is usually disclosed to solicitors, all discussions and negotiations are private (or 'privileged'). The aim of mediation is to work towards a written Memorandum of Understanding setting out the points which have been resolved. This document will be prepared by the mediators and will also be private. The fact that it is 'privileged' means that it cannot be shown to a court; neither spouse is bound by the terms until each has had the chance to take independent advice from a solicitor. It is then shown to each spouse's solicitor. At that point you can obtain your solicitor's comments. If you are happy with the agreement, one or other solicitor may draft a detailed Deed of Separation, or an order for the court to make in the terms agreed. If solicitors are used in this consultative way during the mediation process there is likely to be less need to adjust the terms agreed in the order.

(D) Advantages and Disadvantages of Mediation

Mediation involves a high degree of commitment on the part of all involved. It is not an easy process. It is often emotional and requires forbearance on both sides if the process is to move forward.

The Government believes that greater use of mediation will help it achieve its objectives under the new law. These objectives are as follows:

– to help separating and divorcing couples reach their own agreed, joint decisions about future arrangements;
– to improve communications between them; and
– to help couples work together on the practical consequences of divorce, with particular emphasis on joint responsibilities to co-operate as parents in bringing up their children.

By giving its backing to mediation, the Government hopes that clear advantages will be gained by those families involved in divorce, and that the underlying philosophy behind mediation will minimise the conflict of those involved.

So if you are involved in this process, what are the main advantages?

(1) Advantages

(a) Control: With mediation there should be a greater ability to control the course of the divorce and avoid the need for court proceedings which will impose their own timetable. Both spouses are giving the facts simultaneously and fully, using language which is familiar rather than legal jargon.

(b) Acceptance: Acceptance of what you have negotiated should come more easily, for it will have been something you have participated in, usually with a great deal of effort, with both sides' needs and interests heard and then acknowledged as the best outcome. While reluctance may remain, you will have rejected the alternatives and will feel you have participated in choosing a plan or plans.

(c) Cost: Mediation is not free, but mediators sometimes do not have the same level of overheads as solicitors. Even when a solicitor–mediator is involved, the expense is likely to be less than the adversarial system with two solicitors handling a divorce from start to finish. Even if not all the issues can be agreed in mediation, much of the preparatory work for the respective solicitors will have been done in advance. This in itself will save on solicitors' fees.

(d) Timing: The mediation process can be paced in a way that suits the participants, giving them more control over the process. Divorce proceedings may more easily be postponed while interim arrangements are considered and put in place.

(e) Help in discussing potentially difficult matters: Skilled mediators are there to help you manage to introduce and then sort through topics which many divorcing couples are too frightened to speak about directly to each other. The managed discussion of necessary and mutually vital topics may be the single most valuable contribution of mediation. The ability to talk through these issues directly can save couples potentially great amounts of time and money, rather than if they had to instruct solicitors to handle things for them.

(f) Avoids adversarial positions being taken too quickly: when solicitors negotiate matters, inevitably they express one partial point of view with the expectation that the other point of view is going to be expressed by the other solicitor. In these circumstances it is often the case that points of view are expressed in a hostile or aggressive manner. As a result of this, positions can become entrenched quickly and views can become polarised. In mediation it is possible to avoid this polarisation more easily, because the parties hear from each other directly, without legal language being used or views being expressed in ways which might create a misunderstanding.

(2) Potential Disadvantages of Mediation

(a) Emotional exhaustion: After a particularly fraught session of mediation many wish they had instructed a solicitor to do the negotiating for them, for it is undeniably difficult to confront your soon to be ex-spouse face-to-face when you are both emotionally overwrought.

(b) Difficulty in keeping objectivity: If you are involved directly in negotiations you are unlikely to keep an objective perspective on the significance of the issues under discussion. Much then depends on the skill of your mediators in keeping this perspective alive. An example of this is when discussing contact arrangements. If you will be inconvenienced by your ex-husband having an extra day during the week to spend with your children, and if you think you are the more responsible parent yet you know that the children would like an extra day, and their father is keen to have it, it might be difficult to see past your own inconvenience and prejudices and agree that it would be better for the children to have increased time with him.

(c) Difficulty in achieving balance in negotiations for both parties: All mediators should be aware of the difficulties that can arise if a couple carry power-plays from their own relationship into mediation. For example, if one of the couple characteristically dominates, it is difficult in mediation to redress this imbalance to get the other to speak up, to fight his or her own corner. Women, in particular, often feel they are in a less powerful position to negotiate, especially over finances. Mediators, as a group, have been made aware of this potential gender power imbalance. If there has been a background of violence, mediation is probably unsuitable because of the fear that will permeate. Where there is an imbalance, however, the mediators must be skilled and experienced enough to ensure equality of negotiation. It is vital that each party's voice is heard, and indeed feels that it has been heard.

(d) Duration: Mediation can be laborious, and so is a potentially slow process. For example, one or both of those involved may urgently want to buy a house, yet the urgency may be at odds with other issues being addressed in mediation.

(e) Does it achieve the 'best settlement'?: One of the criticisms of mediation is that a settlement reached ultimately may not be as good for either of the participants as would be negotiated by two individual solicitors. In the process of giving and taking, not all the issues may have been highlighted and brought out sufficiently. Critics say that the mediation process puts too great an emphasis on reaching a settlement, rather than on reaching a settlement that deals thoroughly with all the needs of all parties, both now and in the future.

It should be remembered that solicitors, who are ultimately instructed after the mediation process, can deal with any areas that remain outstanding. The couple may be reluctant, though, after the hard work of mediation, to consider fresh issues and may be disinclined to refine any aspect that has been laboriously negotiated, for fear of being seen to be reneging on the terms reached. Yet, in the end, mediation is only a consultative process which enables suggestions, rather than hard-line recommendations, to be made. Seen in this way, mediation is not a final but a potentially constructive part of the way forward in divorce for a family.

Ultimately the success of any negotiation, whether in mediation or through solicitors, depends upon the attitude of those involved. It is important to know what objectives are imperative, and whether these can be realistically achieved. If either party remains obstinate it will probably lead to the courtroom, whether negotiations have started within mediation or through solicitors.

It may be helpful to have some knowledge of the background of the organisations involved. There are currently two main organisations which train and supervise those involved in mediation. Although the organisations are presently working towards common standards and a common code of practice, there are still some differences.

1 **National Family Mediation** This evolved out of a separate organisation, the National Family Conciliation Council (NFCC). Originally its role was restricted to dealing with issues about children, such as contact difficulties. Usually a mediator from this organisation is from a profession specialising in emotional issues facing families. However, increasingly over the last five years their mediators have been trained to deal with financial issues as well. When a mediator deals with both finances and children, this is referred to as 'comprehensive mediation'.

2 **The Family Mediators Association** This body is different in that one of the mediators involved in any session will be a solicitor or barrister specialising in family law, while the other is from a profession specialising in handling families' emotional issues (such as a social worker, psychologist, family therapist, Court Welfare Officer, psychiatrist or psychotherapist). This organisation has always been able to offer help in dealing with both children's and financial issues. While mediators do not advise, it is possible to draw upon the lawyer's experience as a source of information, be it about legal proceedings or questions of law, or upon the psychological expertise of the other professional involved.

9

DEALING WITH A SOLICITOR

(A) Choosing a Solicitor

Almost everyone knows someone who has been through a divorce. Recommendations from others is the best route to choosing a solicitor. Recommendations should lead to a short-list. They should include information about the approach a solicitor takes and whether the person who has recommended him or her found this approach constructive or not. Solicitors are trained to represent one person's interests against another's. They will put forward arguments and points of view in a way that sometimes exacerbates tensions between a couple. But a good solicitor will fight your corner without creating unnecessary ill-feeling. Asking people who have used a solicitor's services how sympathetic, constructive and reliable he or she was is the best guide to whether a given solicitor will be right for you.

Sometimes a blunt, brisk approach to negotiations is needed. There are cases where the mistrust in one or other of the parties is well founded. In particularly entrenched cases, using the legal process may be your only route to a settlement. It is likely to be costly, but if proceedings are handled skilfully the expenses can be kept down. Indeed, if obstruction can be shown it is sometimes possible to recover some legal expenses from the spouse who has been shown to be so.

The hallmark of a good solicitor is his or her ability to control negotiations and the legal process. This is different to dominating the negotiations; it is important to remember that the solicitor is there to take your instructions; you are the client and you should therefore be fully informed as to the issues involved. Rather, the question of control is one of keeping the momentum going so that negotiations do not get bogged down, of clarifying the issues involved and being creative in resolving them, and in ensuring that everybody moves purposefully towards a fair settlement.

The whole area of family law is becoming increasingly specialised. There are obvious benefits in choosing a solicitor who specialises in this area. Such a solicitor will be used to dealing with the complex issues that arise and should be better equipped to find constructive solutions when negotiating. There is a tendency for solicitors who do not specialise to go to barristers for a second opinion; the cost of doing so will add to their fees.

In the end, the solicitor you appoint should ideally have the same judgement about issues as you, be it in how to handle these issues, how to get the best out of the legal process or how to work flexibly with mediators.

(B) The Solicitors Family Law Association – Code of Practice

The Solicitors Family Law Association (SFLA) has some 3,500 members nationally, all of whom subscribe to its Code of Practice. The aim of the Association is to promote a conciliatory atmosphere and deal with matters in a sensitive, constructive and cost-effective way.

The Code of Practice is designed to reduce the animosity in divorce. The Law Society recommends that all solicitors practising family law should follow the Code of Practice, even those who are not members of the Association, and the Code has also been given judicial approval.

Some of the main objects of the Code are:

– that the solicitor should encourage the parties to achieve a constructive settlement of their differences as quickly as may be reasonable, whilst recognising that the parties may need time to come to terms with their new situation;
– the solicitor should encourage the attitude that a family dispute is not a contest in which there is one winner and one loser, but rather a search for fair solutions;
– in all dealings, the solicitor should avoid taking any action which is likely to cause or increase animosity between the parties;
– the solicitor should aim to promote co-operation between parents in decisions concerning any children;
– issues to do with children should be kept separate from any issues about finance.

Within such a large organisation there will obviously be a range of experience and expertise. It does not necessarily follow that solicitors who are members of the SFLA specialise exclusively in family law. Nonetheless, when choosing a solicitor the question of whether he or she adheres to the Code of Practice may be important to bear in mind.

(C) How Best to Use Your Solicitor

Most solicitors charge for legal work on an hourly basis. You should ask a solicitor what his or her hourly rate is and whether this includes a 'mark-up' for general care and conduct and whether or not it is inclusive or exclusive of VAT and disbursements. Your solicitor is required to give full details of his or her terms of engagement; you can ask for these if they are not volunteered.

Because solicitors' overheads are high their time will be expensive. To save money all that can be done to save solicitors' time should be done. If asked for information or documents it saves time and therefore money if a quick and detailed response can be given, or if you track documents down yourself, for example.

It is easy to forget that a solicitor takes instructions from his or her client. It is desirable for you as the client to take responsibility for what goes on. Solicitors will, if asked, produce letters in draft before they are sent. Given that most solicitors will copy letters from the other spouse's legal representative to their client, it is important that you are in charge – that you make sure that these are not written in a way that you think is likely to cause offence or misunderstanding. You can ask a solicitor to modify things about which you are uncomfortable.

It is helpful to make a list of questions you wish to ask your solicitor before each meeting or phone call with him or her. This helps you to make best use of your solicitor's time, avoiding the expense of numerous telephone calls on separate points.

As negotiations develop there will be increasing paperwork. If legal proceedings are under way this level of organisation can be critical in achieving the objectives being pursued. Keeping this organised, with a good filing system, can also cut down on time and solicitors' expenses.

All such documents and correspondence are highly confidential and should be kept locked away from other family members. Correspondence from your solicitor might have to be sent away from the family home, to a post office box or a different address.

People frequently turn to their solicitors for advice on the emotional fall-out from separation and divorce, or as sounding boards for their anger or desperation. Since your solicitor is the one other person apart from your family intimately connected with your divorce, this tendency is understandable. Moreover, your solicitor is by definition your advocate. In a situation as polarised as divorce, turning to your advocate to complain at length about your adversary is also understandable, although if what you are seeking is help, guidance or advice about how to live with your anger or devastation, or how best to approach your spouse so you can move through your divorce more smoothly, your solicitor is not necessarily the expert to whom you should turn. Above all, he or she is an expensive choice for this; moreover a solicitor is not one who possesses appropriate expertise. Many solicitors now recognise this, and enlightened ones may recommend a consultation with a counsellor or therapist if they feel you might benefit from this advice.

10

FINANCIAL PROCEEDINGS

(A) Why Are Financial Proceedings Necessary?

There are three main areas of potential legal dispute when people are divorcing:

(1) whether or not to divorce (and if so when);
(2) arrangements for children;
(3) financial arrangements.

Disputes most often arise over finances.

Finances are a complicated area and misunderstandings will thus be likely. They are also the area in which opposing interests are seen most starkly.

In earlier chapters we've seen that it is most helpful to let the trauma of early separation settle down before tackling longer-term decisions, although this may not always be possible. Couples are often launched by circumstances into difficult negotiations while still coming to terms with the distress of the initial separation, so they are not in the best position to be even partially objective. Inevitably such negotiations can be quite acrimonious. There may even be a greater chance of financial proceedings commencing without regard to the expense or possibility of fully exploring the middle ground.

Despite this, the vast majority of couples settle all questions, including those about money, without having to have a contested court hearing. It is cheaper to settle 'out of court', and the unpleasantness of litigating (that is to say fighting through the courts) can then be avoided.

When solicitors are involved it is normal to give information about the individual's financial position in correspondence. This is the process called 'disclosure' that has been described in Chapter 5. It is also usual for solicitors to put proposals for settlement in letters, to avoid the need to go to court.

When the couple attend mediation, this process may deal with disclosure and collecting the financial information which can later be passed to the solicitors.

The negotiations themselves will nearly always be private, or 'privileged' – with letters being written and conversations being conducted on a 'without prejudice' basis. This is so whether negotiations are through solicitors or in mediation. The reason for this is to enable the couple to explore ways of settling their differences; the content of these 'without prejudice' discussions cannot be shown to a court if the case does have to go to trial, so the couple are able to make proposals more freely.

However constructively a couple may try to resolve their differences, it may not be possible to do so. It may be genuinely necessary for a court to adjudicate upon a particular point to do with maintenance or capital. This does not invalidate the process of mediation or the attempts by any solicitor to negotiate a settlement. The fewer number of issues which have to be considered by a court, the more straightforward the proceedings will be. As a result, the legal costs will be lower.

Sometimes, formal applications to the court are made because one or the other spouse is not being candid about his or her financial position. Although each individual has a duty to the court to give the fullest possible description of his or her financial position, this is not always done. If so, the other spouse will have no alternative but to use the court procedures to force certain points of information to be provided or certain documents to be produced. One of the purposes of litigation (that is, asking the courts to determine a dispute) is to ensure that all the information is given, so that those involved and the court itself can consider the whole picture.

The questions which have to be addressed by any family on the verge of marital breakdown are going to be difficult. It is easy to see that some questions are going to create conflict, and within that conflict there may be a real reluctance to co-operate, be it in giving information or in putting forward constructive proposals. Again, the question of when these questions are addressed can be critical.

For example, if a wife is left for another woman it may be many months before she is able to consider questions of long-term housing or pensions. In these circumstances her husband may be long used to the idea of a separation, having thought the matter through months before the separation occurred. It is easy for him to begin to feel impatient as the months pass without any prospect of the legal issues being resolved.

When negotiations do begin, the wife's solicitor may be keen to learn about his pension rights or other aspects of his financial life – or even his new partner's financial life – which he did not think would be relevant. He in turn may view savings which his wife has received from an inheritance as forming part of the family assets which need to be considered. These sort of details may be only grudgingly referred to, and full details of them may be refused.

There is no justification in refusing to provide financial details where these are relevant, but the emotional context can make such questions seem very unfair. Much depends on the skill of the mediators or the solicitors who are conducting the negotiations, to ensure that the relevance of such questions is explained and justified.

Where there is a refusal to give financial information, just as much as where there is an issue which genuinely cannot be resolved by discussion, there may be no alternative but to apply to the courts for help.

Where proceedings are being conducted through the court, we do recommend that a solicitor is involved. At the very least it is important to take advice, even if only on a consultancy basis, before embarking on what is a technically difficult process. The purpose of this chapter is to ensure that you understand what the issues and basic procedures are. This will help you to give instructions to your solicitor.

(B) What Are Financial Proceedings?

The purpose of financial proceedings is to get a judge to make an order dealing with the various financial issues and with all the legal rights of each of the parties.

When a full financial settlement is agreed, either during financial proceedings or without the need to issue them, it will still be advisable to obtain an order of the court. This is because, effectively, an order will provide judicial approval of the terms that are agreed and the means to enforce those terms. It will also ensure that there is finality and that no further claims can be dealt with. In Chapter 5 we looked at the menu of orders that a court can make. Normally a court would make all of these orders, or at least dismiss the claims for capital if such claims are not necessary. Only occasionally will a court allow capital (financial) claims to remain open.

It is also important to remember that orders for maintenance can always be reconsidered and changed. The capital orders, for the sale of a home or for the payment of a lump sum of money, are 'one-off' orders – that is, they can only be made once.

When there are contested proceedings a formal application will have been made to the court, so that the court can then set a timetable for the conduct of the matter through to a final hearing.

When proceedings for divorce or judicial separation have begun it is normal to have any financial agreement written directly into an order of the court. When there are no proceedings for divorce or judicial separation it will not be possible to ask the court to make a financial order and so a Deed of Separation will be the only choice for setting out the agreed terms in a formal way.

(1) The Application and the Affidavit

Either party can apply to the court for financial issues to be addressed. It does not matter whether a particular spouse is the petitioner or the respondent in divorce proceedings; this will have no bearing on the financial proceedings.

It is possible to get Legal Aid to cover the costs of financial proceedings. Applying for Legal Aid involves being means-tested, and only those on modest incomes or those who are particularly badly in debt will be eligible. It is important to remember, too, that Legal Aid works as a loan, not as an outright gift and must be paid back, if capital (in other words assets property or lump sums of money) is recovered by the proceedings or is retained as a result of them. You can defer repayment if you are buying property with the lump sum, although additional interest will then be payable.

The initial application to the court for matters of finance to be considered will be started by a formal application. This will be accompanied by a sworn statement called an 'affidavit', which will set out all the personal and financial details of both the person making the application and the family as a whole. The court will be directed to the various considerations set out in the Matrimonial Causes Act (these have already been referred to). The court will also be directed in the affidavit as to what particular orders it is being asked to make, and what particular issues are being addressed.

The courts are very keen that affidavits strike the right balance between giving all the relevant information on the one hand and being succinct on the other. Only rarely will the behaviour of one or other spouse be relevant, and then only in extreme circumstances. Being openly critical or hostile of the other spouse is more likely to work against the spouse making the claims than the reverse.

The application and the affidavit in support of it, together with any documents which are attached or 'exhibited' to the affidavit, are then sent to the solicitor acting for the other party. An affidavit is made in reply, again setting out the financial details of that spouse and replying to the questions of issue which are raised.

When preparing these initial affidavits it is important that both the solicitors and the clients know precisely what they are asking the court to do. The affidavit lays the foundation for the case, and the future design of the proceedings is very much dependent upon it. The courts do not encourage parties to file additional affidavits unless this is made necessary by further issues being raised or new information coming to hand.

This is why it is usual for solicitors to correspond and to discuss both the financial information and the issues beforehand.

(2) Disclosure of Additional Information

After the initial affidavits have been filed at the court and sent to the other parties involved, it is possible to ask for additional financial information. This can be done in the form of a 'questionnaire'; if information is not volunteered the courts can be asked to order that this information be produced.

The solicitors conducting the case can apply during the course of financial proceedings for additional orders. These can be made at short court hearings, known as 'directions hearings', which may last 10 or 20 minutes. During such a hearing the solicitor will address the court on particular questions which may concern the production of documents and whether these are relevant. Courts can and usually will make orders about expert evidence being supplied. This is dealt with in more detail below (*see page 122*).

Increasingly the courts are taking a more positive role in making sure that proceedings are conducted in a constructive and business-like way. Judges are directed to make sure that the evidence for which it is being asked is appropriate to the issues involved. At every stage during the proceedings the question of legal costs should be borne in mind, as these can escalate substantially. It is good practice for any solicitor involved in such proceedings to advise his or her client about the costs that have arisen on a regular basis.

(3) Expert Evidence

Because large sums of money are at stake, and because of the importance to the long-term interests of each member of the family, it is important to be sure of the facts upon which you are relying. For example, if it is assumed that the house can be sold for a particular figure it is important that such an assumption is correct. For this reason, many of those involved in financial proceedings obtain experts in a particular field to give evidence.

It is quite common to ask for a valuer to say how much a particular house or other property is worth. Some estate agents will value a property without charge if it is likely to be sold. It may also be that a single valuer can be instructed by both parties in the case, to keep the costs of having such an expert to a minimum. However, this may cause additional problems, outweighing the relatively small financial benefit. If only one expert is instructed, the parties will be bound by the evidence that is given. This may not be palatable, particularly if the valuation is not a straightforward one. Also, it may be difficult to agree upon the choice of valuer. But if one spouse puts forward expert evidence on a valuation and the other decides not to, then there may be real problems in contradicting the evidence put forward.

All these are issues which should be discussed with the solicitor conducting the case.

Other experts may be called upon to give evidence about pension rights, about family businesses or about the value of other assets, including investments. With all these experts, the question of paying them and the question of the increase in the costs of the court case are going to be crucial and must be weighed up against the potential benefits to be gained. Experts are expensive.

Where possible, the courts are very keen to ensure that the expert evidence is agreed as much as possible before any final hearing. This can reduce the time which the case takes in the court and also simplify the issues involved. It may be that the expert evidence can be agreed in advance, or at least the difference between the two positions narrowed to the point where it will not be necessary for the experts to attend court.

(4) The Final Hearing

Throughout the financial proceedings the solicitors involved will normally be attempting to settle the case through negotiation. As the case progresses, so the legal costs will increase and become central to the overall settlement. For this reason it is important to keep legal costs under a tight rein.

In some cases legal costs may begin to outweigh, in a commercial sense, the financial issues being disputed. It is for this reason that the Government is keen to promote a more cost-effective way of negotiating settlements through mediation. However, the individuals involved may decide that since the final outcome of the case is going to affect their financial lives long into the future, increased cost is not an issue.

Once a date has been fixed for a final hearing at which the judge will hear and determine the issues, it is necessary to prepare the evidence that is going to go before the court. This will involve copies of all the relevant documents being taken and put into files. Doing this enables the judge to have all the relevant information at hand.

If a hearing is to decide questions of property it will probably last for at least a day. More complicated cases are 'set down' for longer periods than that. It is likely that the hearing date will be given some months in advance. Although this is because the courts are so busy, it also gives time to prepare for a hearing and to see if a settlement can still be reached by negotiation.

Part of the preparation for a hearing will probably be instructing a barrister. It is usually advisable to have a meeting with a barrister beforehand to discuss the case. Such meetings are called conferences. This gives you, the client, an opportunity to discuss points of particular concern with the barrister, and ensures that the barrister has a deeper understanding of the case.

Barristers are used because they are experts at presenting cases to the court. They may also have a more specialised knowledge of the legal issues involved. In particular, the barrister will probably know which way the court is likely to consider the evidence and tackle the questions that are being raised.

The solicitors involved will try to negotiate a settlement right up to the hearing, even at the door of the court itself. If each spouse instructs a barrister, negotiations can be carried out by them.

The run-up to a trial or hearing is stressful and pressurised. Negotiations become intense and it is during this stage that the solicitor will show his or her true worth. To a certain extent barristers take over the running of the case once they are instructed, saying what in their view would be an appropriate settlement and how the case should be conducted in court. But it is the solicitor who is at the centre of it, and you as the client will be placing enormous reliance on his or her understanding and objectivity. This is why the choice of solicitor is so important.

Both parties usually give evidence at a hearing. This involves answering questions about legal issues raised and about future plans. Each spouse will be asked questions both by his or her own barrister and by the other barrister, whose questions will be more challenging and perhaps even aggressive.

Some couples leave the courtroom frustrated and angry, feeling that they did not have a chance to 'have their say'. But the court is there only to consider evidence being presented. That evidence may only be designed to deal with quite narrow questions of fact. The court gives a decision based upon these questions. It is not there to comment on the behaviour of one spouse nor to 'punish' him or her in any way. It is purely the means of adjudicating certain issues.

The process of litigation, of going through the courts, takes a heavy toll both emotionally and financially. It takes many months and will dominate the lives of all those involved. It is difficult coming to terms with the psychological pressures involved, and these are very likely to affect other family members, including children. This adversarial system, with its opposing legal positions, produces conflict by its very nature. It therefore requires a degree of detachment from those taking part. There has to be a balance between negotiating a sensible settlement, especially in the face of mounting legal fees, and giving way to psychological pressure or emotional bullying.

Before beginning financial proceedings it is always best to state very clearly what it is you are trying to achieve. The cost of achieving that goal, in terms of legal fees, should also be brought into the equation. There is no point in spending £5,000 on legal fees where the difference between the respective positions only amounts to some £10,000. Most solicitors will advise their clients to take a pragmatic approach and compromise on practical areas, rather than fighting a crusade of principle at vast expense. It is never easy to compromise given the emotional context of marital breakdown, but enormous expense can be saved and feelings of humiliation and upset avoided.

In the end, the courts can only achieve compromise on financial issues, because the judge has to balance the interests of the parties. It is usually better to try to achieve this compromise in negotiation by being open about disclosure and more flexible in putting forward proposals for settlement.

Finally, whether it is in court or in negotiation, such compromises are always likely to be uncomfortable, or leave one feeling at a disadvantage. But the classic definition of a compromise is a deal that is acceptable to neither party. The likelihood is that both spouses will be feeling much the same.

section 4

CHILDREN AND DIVORCE

11

THE EMOTIONAL IMPACT OF DIVORCE ON CHILDREN

Children do not want divorce in almost every case. Nor do they want to live in unhappy marriages. In children's magical thinking divorce is almost never a solution – deciding to love each other and be kind and happy together is. This is what they want, and it is unlikely that you will at first persuade your child that divorce will be all right for them. They will hurt, they will feel pain, sadness, anger and loss. Limiting the damage of divorce for them should be your aim.

Children do not perceive the breakdown of their parents' relationship in the same terms as their parents. An understanding of children's fundamentally different perspective is crucial in minimising the disturbance they will feel upon marital breakdown. In all age groups the post-divorce relationship between parents and the arrangements made for them are key to whether or not this disturbance is short-lived or enduring.

While one or both parents may decide to end their marriage, they do not end co-parenting. Parents cannot divorce their children. Both psychological research and the legal framework presume that it is in the interests of children to have as extensive a continuing relationship with both parents as possible.

(A) Through the Eyes of a Child

From a growing body of research we can now say some things with certainty about a child's initial responses to the fact of his or her parents' marital breakdown. Chief among these are as follows:

(1) Most children would prefer their parents' marriage to continue, although most have at times considered the marriage to have been unhappy. However, research also tells us that five to six years following a divorce only a small number of children think that their parents were wrong to have divorced.
(2) The hardest stage emotionally for children is just after separation and not necessarily during the unhappy marriage itself.
(3) Children feel shocked, bewildered and lonely when they actually hear the news that their parents are separating or divorcing.
(4) Often children do not understand why their parents have split up. They feel sad at the threat of losing touch with the parent who is leaving.
(5) Children do not know whether the separation is temporary or permanent, which adds to their bewilderment. The bewilderment threatens their sense of security.
(6) However little the parents know of the future, the children know even less.
(7) Children and parents give strikingly different pictures of their feelings and of their comprehension of the reasons for separation.
(8) All children will feel upset, even if they do not say so and even if they do not directly show signs of disturbance.

(B) How Divorce Affects Children

(1) Pre-school Children

Just post-separation, at around two months, both boys and girls often become frightened, confused and clingy. Commonly they become anxious and may also revert to behaviour they have outgrown. They may show aggressive tendencies; this is especially so for boys. They may also become resistant to change. Just after separation boys especially seek out and are more interested in male attention, affection and proximity. Their increase in oppositional and aggressive behaviour can result in isolation and being shunned by their parents and others.

In the first year after separation and divorce, play patterns can become disrupted and less mature. As with behaviour in general, play too may revert to more babyish forms which the children have normally outgrown.

For this age group in particular, although it is true for all ages, a mother's preoccupation with her own depression or other matters may result in disorganisation and lack of control over children in the home. It is possible that this lack of control is associated with such children's behaviour problems, such as distractibility and inattention, both of which have been commonly noted in children following separation. A child's distress feeds on a mother's and vice-versa, and a child's problems may be a manifestation of stresses which a family normally undergoes at this time. In other words, it is normal for children to experience a vicious circle of painful feelings when a family splits up, especially because very young children are not yet old or mature enough to know how to understand, control or voice their feelings.

How Parents Can Help

As well as talking to children honestly, simply and repeatedly about the separation, parents need to try, as far as possible, to retain and be consistent with family rules and routines. Children feel reassured if they know that even though the family is changing, both parents are still paying attention to their behaviour and also continuing with routines. Although it is tempting for parents to be more lenient in disciplining at such a time, out of compassion for their children, it actually makes children feel more secure if parents follow through with discipline. On the other hand, suddenly becoming a harsh disciplinarian, which is a tendency which can arise from stretched patience and feeling overwhelmed, may make children more anxious or frightened. Large changes in routines and expectations for them will be unsettling to children.

When Mike and Linda divorced, Mike, who previously had half-time care of their four-year-old daughter, was very tempted to baby her during the separation process and to indulge her every whim. Where previously he had been firm about bedtimes, eating and disciplining rude behaviour, his impulse was to be the good guy. He dreaded tantrums colouring their time together and feared that she would want to visit him less if she only remembered the struggles. But after a few weeks of her testing his limits, he realised he was not comfortable letting her get away with behaviour he had not previously tolerated – it was affecting the quality of their time together in any case. He returned to his previous style, and she also settled down. Within a short time the wild behaviour and insistent demands, the easy tears from a highly anxious state faded and they resumed their normal, comfortable habits together.

In contrast, Helen became badly depressed, lethargic and overwhelmed after her husband left her with their two small children, aged three and four. She let them eat when they wanted, dispensing with cooking altogether and giving them cereal and biscuits, toast and jam and pizza delivered to the door. She often did not put them to bed, but let them fall asleep in front of the television, carrying them into their beds when she went up to her own. When they fought over toys she let them destroy the toys, resorting to spanking or putting them in their rooms only if one child hurt the other. She managed to get them to nursery each day, but at one point her older son was excluded for a week for uncontrollable behaviour. These children had been used to some order in their lives, some predictability and some rules when their father lived with them; now their sense of what to expect and what was expected of them was utterly confused.

(2) Children 6 to 9

Crying and sadness characterise children in this age group. Missing their departing parent is the most dominant concern of children in this group (this does not mean that younger ones do not feel this, but that they are less likely to have the words and means to say it).

Boys at this age commonly show that they are troubled by one parent's departing by acting out and being more aggressive.

At this age children may also begin to express guilt, as if it is their fault that their marriage is ending. Similarly children at this age may openly urge their parents to reconcile.

How Parents Can Help

Although it may be extremely hard for a parent to do so, it is healthy to allow children to cry and mourn the loss of the family as they know it. Glossing over the sad feelings invalidates them, making a child feel bad or even strange for having them. Moreover, a child who is encouraged to disown his or her sad feelings may begin to resent or withdraw from the parent or parents who encourage this.

Simple phrases such as 'I'm glad that you're telling or showing me how you are feeling' or 'I understand how sad you are at what is happening' or 'everyone feels sad at this time' can be extremely powerful in helping your child accept his or her very normal, inevitable feelings. Parents also need to tell their children that the marriage is not ending because they were bad. Even at this age, children need some explanation of why their parents are breaking up, to help them to accept that it is not their fault. It might be explained in the following way, for instance: 'Mummy and Daddy do not love each other any more; we cannot live together without bad fights but we both love you.' Tell your child that the source of your break-up is you and your relationship rather than him or her.

Sandra and Jonathan had a six-year-old son on whom both doted; he was an only child, although they had tried to conceive, without success, for the first ten years of their marriage. Both desperately wanted children, and even though their marriage had been turbulent and unloving for many years the thought of breaking up had been intolerable because neither could bear to think of parting from their son. Parenting had been split exactly down the middle, as both parents had continued to work after his birth and also had curtailed almost all of their extracurricular activities. Ultimately their marriage broke down after Sandra began an affair with a co-worker and Jonathan found out. The couple went to mediation and agreed to co-parent, dividing the week exactly in half and buying houses within a mile of each other. That was the easy part; the difficult part was telling their son.

They told him together, having agreed a common story beforehand, which contained the emotional truth without the accusatory details. Jonathan began by telling him how much they had wanted to have him, and that this had been the reason they had remained together even though they had begun to stop loving each other, because '... sometimes grown-ups are not very good at not hurting each other and they start to hurt each other so much that they stop being able to get along, and they fight all the time and make each other very unhappy.' Sandra explained that they had thought that they could carry on living together because they both loved him so very much, but they could not, because even though they '... love (him) that much they still make each other cry a lot with unhappiness'. And so they agreed that they could both keep on loving him and being his parents but not being married to each other. He would see Daddy as much as he would see Mummy, but he would live with them in different houses, for some of the week in one, and some in the other, with his own room in both, and they would be near each other, and he could speak to both of them every day.

This was a sad scene; all three cried, the parents quietly, the little boy, very frightened, sobbing. Both parents held, soothed and cuddled him, each allowing the other to show their love for him. Eventually his attention turned to his new Lego, and they let him return to something normal and neutral. They remained careful, gentle, co-operative and polite with each other for the rest of the time they remained necessarily living under the same roof, whenever they were in his presence.

Children at this age and older frequently hope or pray to be extra good so that their parents will get back together. It is important not to foster false hope if there is little chance of reconciliation, or your children will not be able to move on to a new phase in family life. Both telling children that the separation is not their fault and that their parents will not be back together again are crucial to their sense of reality. However, as we have said in Chapter 1, the telling and re-telling need both sensitivity and patience, and the will to repeat and answer questions again and again.

(3) Children 9 to 11

This is the age at which children often become intensely angry at their parents' divorce. Rather than blame themselves they may blame and even reject one of their parents, most commonly the parent with whom they live. Boys more than girls show their anger. In general boys are more likely to become aggressive while girls are more likely to become withdrawn.

Physical symptoms are reported in this age group but, unlike younger children, these children can and do associate these with stressful events, in this case the events surrounding divorce. School performance is often affected as well.

How Parents Can Help

In addition to the ways discussed in the previous sections, the most important way parents can help their children manage their anger is by accepting that they will be angry, as it is a dispersal of their enormous sense of impotence over an event they do not want to happen. This understanding of the root of their anger should give parents the perspective needed to tolerate children's seemingly irrational and frequent outbursts. It is also helpful to realise that anger may seem arbitrary and unconnected directly to the divorce. Anger may be expressed at parents, siblings, friends and even inanimate objects.

Parents' ability to tolerate their children's anger without getting very angry at them in turn may prevent the anger from further spilling out at school or onto siblings. Children often express anger in the place they feel most safe and to the safest person, who is usually their primary carer.

(4) Adolescents

Adolescents also get angry and feel pain at the loss of the family they have known. As they feel more adult, they may prematurely assume adult-like responsibilities, worries and part of the role of the departed parent. They may, for instance, take on worries about the future of the family or the well-being of younger siblings. As a result of their greater maturity, adolescents can identify and talk much better about their parents' divorce and its effects on them. The danger of a child assuming such adult-like burdens is that his or her own sadness, anger and worry are glossed over, and he or she feels unsupported and even emotionally abandoned. This itself can in some cases lead to anger (especially in boys) and withdrawal (especially in girls). Older adolescents also tend to take refuge in sexual relationships, with research showing that children of divorced parents tend to marry younger (and then are more likely themselves to divorce).

By this age it is also the case that children are sometimes relieved when parents separate, because with their greater maturity and sophistication they have seen it as inevitable. Sometimes an adolescent's relationship with one or both parents improves once the parents are living apart. Adolescents do have a greater ability to communicate their feelings and this can mean a stronger bond with their parents during this stressful time. It is sometimes the case that an adolescent can develop a better individual relationship with a parent once the atmosphere of tension or conflict is reduced.

For both boys and girls, school performance often diminishes, as is true for the age group 9 to 11, which can lead to dropping out early from their educational path. Again, research suggests that this can be one effect of divorce.

How Parents Can Help

Again, in addition to what has been pointed out earlier, it is easy to be seduced by a child's apparent ability to help you and to understand, but adolescents still need parents to parent them. These children are frequently the ones most obviously caught in the middle because they become the confidante of one or both parents and feel forced either to take sides or to engage in a constant test of loyalty which they cannot win. Teenagers need to be free of this difficult position. At this stage, also, teenagers usually wish to exercise freedom about visiting or renewing contact with the parent with whom they do not have their primary residence.

It is certainly appropriate for them to have a say in this but, as we argue in Chapter 2, teenagers are still children and cannot be expected to exercise adult judgement over the long-term effects of choosing their social lives over seeing their other parent. In this way parents need to take a long-range view for them, and ensure that they maintain that relationship, unless violence, abuse or other clear damage to a child indicates otherwise.

In their book *Second Chances* the American researchers on divorce Judith Wallerstein and Sandra Blakeslee describe the difficulties the children of divorce have to overcome:

(i) learning to acknowledge the reality of the separation;
(ii) resolving feelings of loss, anger and self-blame;
(iii) being able successfully to disengage from the parental conflict and return to their customary pursuits;
(iv) successfully accepting the permanence of divorce; and
(v) achieving a realistic hope of their own future relationships.

It has been shown that the best post-separation arrangements are those that are flexible, arrived at by agreement between parents, and with children moving easily between both homes.

To help children adapt to separation and divorce, parents need to be aware that the children need to be as free from parental conflicts as possible. Parents also need to acknowledge that, in most cases, it is healthy and important to foster their children's relationship with the other parent. Continued and consistent contact with both parents assists a child in making a good emotional adjustment after the upheaval and insecurity consequent to separation and divorce. Most children do not want to be seen to be rejecting, nor do they want to reject their parent. They should not be put in that role, whether wittingly or unwittingly, by the other parent.

Most children can make a different and often fulfilling relationship with a parent who does not live with them. Most can adapt to such a change if their parents help them by facilitating conditions for them to do so. This underscores the importance of co-operation between parents over their children's relationship with each other, a tall order for people who are not often co-operating or communicating in other ways.

But parents must also acknowledge their limits; there will be times when they find it almost impossible to separate their own feelings from their children's relationships with the other parent. To acknowledge such feelings is not to admit failure, it is instead to recognise the inevitable emotional trauma a parent undergoes no matter whose decision it was to separate.

It is not a failure for parents to seek professional help from therapists or counsellors, whether for themselves alone or their children. Indeed, it may be the wisest and most responsible parent who recognises his or her limits and the value to the family that professional help can give. Again, if divorce is seen as a process in which the trick is to limit damage, intervening at appropriate points with such professional help can be one key step in damage limitation.

A child's suffering must be seen as ongoing in the same way as a parent's distress is, until eventual adjustment is made to a new and settled reality. A child will be upset at partings and reunions. Until he or she has become used to relating to parents separately, in separate households, with separate rules and expectations, until a child can securely expect he or she will be seeing the parent who leaves again, and then will continue to see that parent predictably and regularly, the comings and goings will be times of emotional turmoil and uncertainty. Eventually most children do settle down. Parents must try to achieve this perspective and understanding if they are going to help their children to adjust.

In the same way that it can take an adult a long time to adjust to a change of circumstances of such a fundamental nature, it must also be recognised that it takes at least as much time and emotional energy for a child. This is particularly so since he or she is less likely to understand the grounds for the decision.

(C) Using the Children as Chess Pieces

The tendency for separating couples to need their children is normal. They need assurances of their children's loyalty and love; to reassure children and themselves that the quality or strength of the bond between them will not be affected; and to gain the warmth and reassurance from their children's love during a time when they may feel rejected, on the one hand, or reviled on the other.

When a family splits up, children themselves can feel split. The parents' needs at the time frequently unwittingly encourage further split loyalties. In the case of the spouse who is left, there may be a tendency to need children's reassurance that at least they would never leave. There may also be an inclination to encourage the children to share feelings of rejection or dismay at the departing spouse's behaviour. The person leaving may pressure the children to proclaim particular loyalty or reassurance.

Most people nowadays are aware of the dangers of making children take sides, but they may still do so unwittingly. One manifestation of this is when couples indirectly involve their children in their own battles, by using them as 'chess pieces' to control or subvert their spouse's behaviour. This is seen in manoeuvres such as refusal to pay maintenance on time unless your spouse conforms to a particular demand. It can also be seen in withholding or making contact inconvenient for similar objectives.

Getting information out of children about the other parent is another common example of such behaviour. Children usually know when this occurs. They usually feel used, uncomfortable and 'in the middle'. Prolonged behaviour of this sort can lead to symptoms in the child such as expressions of anger, self-destructive behaviour, depression, withdrawal, truculence or aggressive acting out.

These examples bring up a point that parents often miss during divorce: children sometimes need people other than their parents on whom to lean, to let off steam, to talk to, and with whom to make sense of the changes they are experiencing. They may not want to turn to their parents. Children easily feel they are in the middle, or that they are treading on parents' sensitive feelings or else burdening the very parents about whom they are already so concerned. Instead, people outside the immediate family, such as teachers, friends (especially friends whose parents themselves have divorced), sports coaches, aunts, uncles, grandparents or friends' parents may fill this role.

Younger children may have these feelings as well. They will not, however, have the resources; they cannot decide to turn to others for help. And many children, no matter their age or the scope of their social network, may find it impossible to turn to someone outside the family. Some will feel even this to be a breach of loyalty.

(D) Counselling for Children

In such cases it may be helpful to give children an opportunity to consult a counsellor who specialises in working with children of separating or divorcing parents. Rather than stigmatising a child or symbolising a parent's failure to handle his or her child, this should be seen as a farsighted parental action. From what we now know about divorce, counselling is a potentially invaluable way to speed up a child's adjustment and again a way to limit potential damage; to 'manage' the effects of divorce. In most cases a single or a few consultations can help.

Emma was a 10-year-old whose parents were going through a messy divorce. Neither would speak to the other, except to make cursory contact arrangements, with most communication going through lawyers or Emma. Angry messages would be left on the answer machine for her mother from her father, and her mother would use Emma as a messenger for enraged notes she would stuff in her daughter's pockets as she left to see her father.

Emma was a compliant, quiet child, but her teachers noticed a distinct change. She was distracted and uncommunicative at school and her work became careless. Since the school knew about the parents' imminent divorce they suggested that Emma see the school counsellor specially recruited because of the high incidence of divorce in the area. At first Emma resisted, as she felt to talk about her situation would mean disloyalty to her parents, but gradually the counsellor gained her trust and she began to open up. She hated most 'being in the middle'. The counsellor found out that Emma could identify a feeling '... in my stomach' (and she pointed to just where she felt it) when she felt she was being put in the middle. It happened when '... Daddy is pumping me, asking me questions about Mummy, like how much she spends on things, or what she spends her time doing' and she felt it when '... Mummy asks me what Daddy's house is like, and what photos he has up, and whether anyone phones him when I'm there, and how much money he spends on me when he takes me out.' She also felt it when '... either of them starts to complain about the other one. It's like they expect me to agree and to say how horrible the other one is, and I just go all quiet and shut up and I feel terrible. That is the worst.'

'Going quiet' is what Emma resorted to under the pressure of 'being in the middle'. She went quiet but the terrible feelings persisted and they stayed with her, under the pressure to be a good daughter to both parents and as she suffered the desperate dilemma of loving both so much and feeling that by doing so she could not support either. These feelings dominated so that she could not concentrate, and yet she still remained 'quiet'. Luckily for her, her school gave her a place in which she could stop being 'quiet' and let the feelings out and try to understand them. These sessions gave her an invaluable way of letting them out and feeling better about herself. She eventually learned ways, with the help of the counsellor, to tell her parents when she felt 'in the middle' so that they backed off. She also began to relax and concentrate, so school and friends were restored to being a 'conflict-free zone' and she had more emotional reserves for home.

While many people turn to the private sector for this, there are some voluntary or non-profit centres in some communities which offer such services at very little or nominal expense. Cambridge, for instance, has a pioneering programme at its Family and Divorce Centre, as does the Institute for Family Therapy in London. In a number of towns there is a contact centre for parents who need a neutral place for collecting children at contact visits.

Child psychiatry departments and mediation centres are increasingly offering different forms of counselling for both parents and children, or the whole family together; i.e. family counselling, couple, individual or children's counselling. Enquiries can be made via GPs, local child psychiatry departments, mediation services (and family divorce centres), social services, court welfare offices, step-family associations and, increasingly, via solicitors.

When a divorcing couple manage to separate their dispute from their parental role, and can agree on the best ways to meet their children's needs, then children have a greater chance of getting on with their development. It can, however, take anything from three to five years to recover from divorce-generated upheaval. In addition, latent influences of the divorce process can appear many years later, when the child reaches a vulnerable stage of development, such as adolescence. As we said in Chapter 1 this is seen particularly in the fact that children whose parents have divorced form their own sexual relationships earlier on, marry earlier, have a higher than average incidence of divorce themselves, achieve lower than expectable school performances and leave school earlier.

However, it should be noted that it is notoriously difficult for anyone to separate the effects of divorce from other problems, such as poverty, poor parental relationship prior to divorce, a grandparent's death, emigration or illness, any of which may occur around or after the time of divorce. It is important to remember that sometimes divorce can be better for children than parents' staying together conflictually and miserably. Making divorce the scapegoat for all or any symptoms children might display obscures this perspective. So does portraying divorce as a process from which children must inevitably suffer for the indefinite future.

It is important to emphasise that most children adapt given above all their parents' co-operation and attention to their welfare. Most children recover and go on to live happy and productive lives. Most have rewarding relationships.

However, it is also true to say that in the short term children do experience divorce as a trauma. How well they cope and are enabled to cope with these feelings also contribute to their long-term development. As we have said above, to enable this coping in the short term many children do benefit immeasurably from having someone outside, a counsellor for instance, to help them manage their deeply painful and confusing emotions. Such help should be seen as a potentially enormous investment in their future adjustment and a wise way that parents can help in managing the divorce process.

Recognising the emotional upheaval of divorce for all parties has resulted in the fact that many more people seek counselling for themselves and for their children. Sometimes parents, singly or even together, can be helped to enable their children's adjustment, as well as their own, by themselves seeing a professional. This is especially true if that professional has expertise in treating families. Consultation with such experts can help a parent both understand and gain skills in managing a child's sometimes baffling or overwhelming behaviour. Sometimes just getting help for managing and understanding your own feelings and behaviour through counselling or therapy can be the route to helping your children.

Children, depending on their age, may experience difficulties in one or more of the following spheres and, if so, intervention by an expert might be helpful.

(a) *Emotional difficulties:* symptoms will depend on age but may be any of these: anxiety (especially anxiety over separation), grief and depression, self-blame, anger, as well as overly adult 'too good' behaviour (i.e. a change to being overly compliant, too quiet, too helpful and too watchful of what parents want them to do and say)
(b) *Social difficulties:* isolation and withdrawal from others, increased aggression and destructiveness (especially boys), sexual 'acting out'
(c) *Educational difficulties:* decrease in academic performance, poor concentration, increased aggression in school, changes in ability to communicate with teachers and/or peers, withdrawal from others
(d) *Health problems:* emotional stress can sometimes be expressed as a physical illness. Additionally, if a child already has a chronic illness the difficulties experienced with the complaint may increase.

Counselling can enhance children's coping abilities and it may prevent or ameliorate these difficulties. Facilities available will vary depending on where you live, but they are growing, as it is (and should be) becoming more normal and acceptable to get psychological help during divorce.

12

THE LEGAL FRAMEWORK RELATING TO CHILDREN

(A) 'Parental Responsibility'

When parents are married at the time of a child's birth, or if they marry subsequently, both have 'parental responsibility' for that child. This concept was introduced by the Children Act 1989. It replaces the old concept of 'custody', which no longer exists.

Parental responsibility is defined in the Children Act as 'all the rights, duties, powers, responsibilities and authority which by law a parent of a child has in relation to the child and his property'. Either parent can operate this individually and can also delegate it to others, as appropriate.

This concept, 'parental responsibility', arose out of an increasing emergence of children's rights, as opposed to those of parents. It is a child's right, for instance, to have contact with both parents. It is also a child's right to have his or her best interests protected by his or her parents. When parents are unable to fulfil that role or to meet a child's needs the State will intervene, protecting the child's rights. When parents cannot agree how a child's best interests are served a court will determine the issue, again to protect the child's rights.

As a child gets older he or she is thought to become more and more able to make certain decisions for him or herself. Therefore parental authority increasingly diminishes as a child grows. The specific responsibilities which any parent has will change as needs and circumstances differ, and also will vary with the age and maturity of a child.

The assumption now is that once children are 16 they are able to make all decisions for themselves. Once 16, the general principle is that neither the parents, the State nor the courts can intervene in decisions about his or her welfare. However, parental responsibility does not formally lapse until a child is 18, the legal age of maturity.

On a practical basis, issues involved in parental responsibility comprise all those relating to a child's upbringing, including where that child is to live, with whom he or she is to have contact, and all matters relating to that child's health and education.

(B) Can Arrangements Be Agreed?

Upon divorce or separation both parents will continue to have parental responsibility for a child. This change of emphasis promotes what we know to be true: a child will adjust better if parents can co-operate well after separation and divorce, and if a child has a good degree of contact with both parents.

Since the introduction of the Children Act in October 1991, the law presumes that on divorce the court will make no orders governing arrangements for any children. Therefore no automatic order is made upon divorce, although a Statement of Arrangements for Children form (*see Chapter 7*) is filed at court. This sets out practical details which relate to the children's welfare. The court can investigate them further if not happy with the arrangements. In practice it will rarely do so. The court will only make an order if it is satisfied that it is in the child's best interests for there to be an order.

The premise for this change in law was based on the fact that if parents can co-operate, they will know what is most workable for them both. If an agreement can be reached between them it is obviously much more likely to be successful in the long term. In such cases, courts will therefore never need to become involved in these arrangements. The term 'custody' was abolished in order to neutralise what was frequently a very bitter battle: custody being regarded as a trophy to be won at all costs.

The types of decisions to be made concerning a child on divorce will need to cover both where a child is to live and also how much contact he or she will have with the other parent. It may be agreed that the child shall spend an equal amount of time with each parent. Research has shown that in fact equal time is the best situation for children, with the following very important provisos: parents should be free of conflict around their children and should live near enough to each other so that the children's day-to-day social and educational lives can run smoothly and easily.

However, such a shared care arrangement will only work where parents retain a co-operative co-parenting relationship, and sadly, this is unlikely always to be the case, despite the best intentions and efforts of all involved, given the painful process of divorce.

Other decisions which will be necessary concerning the child may relate to schooling or medical treatment. Each parent can take a necessary decision individually, but issues of a serious matter should be discussed and agreed in advance by both parents, at least in principle. If an agreement can be reached there is no need for outside agencies to become involved, therefore avoiding the cost and emotional upheaval of such involvement.

Parents will also perhaps need to liaise about travelling abroad. This is examined in Chapter 13.

(C) Outside Intervention

There will be some situations in which parents cannot agree about arrangements for their children. If matters cannot be resolved between parents, either directly or through mediation, either parent, or a child if he or she is old enough, can make an application to the court to resolve the issue. At this point it is extremely important to get legal advice, if you have not already done so, although it is possible for an individual to act for him or herself.

(1) The Welfare Principle

The central precept of the Children Act is that the child's welfare is the court's paramount consideration when looking at any question with respect to a child's upbringing. Put another way, the job of the court is to seek to determine what is in a child's best interests. In so doing the court will take a number of prescribed factors into account.

These are set out in a check-list, which the following summarises:

- the ascertainable wishes and feelings of the child concerned (considered in the light of the child's age and understanding);
- the child's physical, emotional and educational needs;
- the likely effect on the child of any change in circumstances (including consideration of the status quo);
- the child's age, sex, background and any characteristics of the child which the court considers relevant (for instance, religion or race);
- any harm which the child has suffered or is at risk of suffering, which is broadly construed and can cover both physical and emotional harm;
- how capable each of the child's parents – and any other person the court considers relevant (for instance, other relatives involved in the child's day-to-day care) – is of meeting the child's needs;

- the range of powers available to the court in the proceedings in question (therefore allowing the court to make any order that it considers appropriate, rather than simply that applied for).

Under the Solicitors Family Law Association (SFLA) Code of Practice, one of the aims is to ensure that any clients appreciate that the interests of children must be the first concern upon relationship breakdown, both in issues specifically relating to children as well as the overall financial arrangements.

An adviser who is a member of the SFLA will very much seek to focus upon the family as a whole and the impact that any decision will have upon relationships between children and their parents. This is an aim set out in the SFLA Code. When separating, it is obviously important that the parent has an adviser with whose approach he or she agrees, but a solicitor who appreciates the importance of children's welfare is likely to be the most helpful if there are children involved.

(2) The Main Types of Orders Available

There are a range of orders a court might make when the State feels it must intervene to protect a child's welfare. However, generally there are four main orders a court may make relating to private disputes following divorce. While these are most often between the parents, the court may also be asked by a child or other adults involved in the child's life, such as grandparents or other relatives, to settle a dispute. In most cases where matters are agreed, a court will decline to make any orders. The types of issues to be considered have already been discussed in earlier chapters, but the four main orders are:

1. Residence (previously 'custody') – an order stating with whom a child is to live. There can be a joint residence order. While this is currently an unusual type of order, it may be that the courts have not yet caught up with current

knowledge that such an order might be best for the children. This might be the case if their parents are able to co-operate over the practical arrangements and if they live near each other.

2. Contact (previously 'access') – an order requiring the person with whom a child lives to allow that child to visit, stay with, or have other contact with a named person (usually the other parent). This can include telephone contact or contact by correspondence.
3. Prohibited Steps – an order prohibiting specific steps taken in relation to a child, for instance prohibiting a change of name or removal from England and Wales.
4. Specific Issue – an order determining a specific issue relating to a child, for example settling a dispute over education or medical treatment.

When a court is to determine an issue relating to children, it starts from the general principle (set out in law) that any delay in resolving the issue is likely to be detrimental to the child's welfare. The court will therefore set out a timetable for the proceedings so that the matter is not allowed to drift and so that the issue is resolved for the child as soon as possible. This is to minimise the inevitable anxiety and insecurity created by court proceedings for all involved, especially the child.

Just because proceedings have been commenced does not mean a full hearing will be necessary. The court will continue to encourage an agreement between those involved. Shortly after the proceedings begin, there will be a short hearing to see whether the matter can be resolved without the need to proceed further. This hearing is also to set out the timetable for the case if an agreement cannot be reached.

Generally at this initial short hearing the parents will have the opportunity to meet with a Court Welfare Officer, either separately or together. This is so they can talk through the areas of dispute with a professional trained in matters of children's welfare, to see whether they can reach an agreement with his or her help. If an agreement cannot be reached, a different Court Welfare Officer will report to the court on the issues under dispute. This Officer will talk to the children in nearly every case. In some areas of Britain, parents will also be offered an appointment with a Court Welfare Officer away from the court, prior to the initial hearing, again to see whether matters can be agreed.

All this is in recognition of the fact that agreed arrangements are more likely to be successful, and also of the fact that protracted proceedings can have an irrevocably damaging effect upon family relationships. In addition, legal proceedings are costly, affecting the resources available to meet a family's housing and financial needs.

If an agreement is reached, the court will not cancel any hearings that have been arranged without satisfying itself that the agreed arrangements are in the children's best interests. However, it would generally not be necessary for the parents to go to court in order for this to be done. Their solicitors will simply inform the court in writing of the agreement.

It is of vital importance throughout any dispute relating to children that it is kept separate from the emotional issues between parents arising out of separation, as well as from any financial negotiations or proceedings. The court will generally treat any proceedings relating to children as entirely separate from any divorce or financial proceedings. This is in order to encourage parents to focus upon the children's needs and to emphasise the continuing nature of the parental relationship. Such an emphasis also seeks to reduce the possibility of children being used as pawns, whether consciously or subconsciously, in disagreements over other issues between the parents.

section 5

THE POST-DIVORCE FAMILY

13

PRACTICAL PROBLEMS FACING THE POST-DIVORCE FAMILY

(A) Children's Ongoing Relationship with Both Parents

Once parents are divorced, just as at the point of separation, children benefit from clear information and expectations about their continuing relationship with both parents. They will be aware that divorce is final and so will wonder if this will mean any change in their day-to-day routine or their contact arrangements. In most cases it will not, but this needs saying and a clear explanation given.

When children are young it is easier to control regular contact. Control over contact arrangements becomes more unwieldy as children form extra-curricular interests which claim their time, and as they get older and develop social lives over which they appropriately expect to exert increasing choice and control. A parent having only, say, weekend contact is understandably very hurt when their children choose to spend time with friends or to attend a school or social event over spending time with him or her. Finding an appropriate, comfortable balance between maintaining regular contact and allowing appropriate social development to occur is the main problem with older children, as is accepting this change as young children get older.

It is appropriate to allow pre-adolescent and adolescent children some say in how they spend their leisure time. However, it is also important to remember that they are still children. That is, they do not have consistently mature judgement. One of the hallmarks of adolescent thinking is a difficulty in projecting into the future with any consistency. Most children, for example, do not have the wisdom to predict that if they keep on choosing social events over seeing their father (usually the parent with whom the children do not have their main home), their relationship with their father will be eroded over time. This is where parents need to take the longer view for them. They need to strike a balance; they should not expect a child, unassisted, to do so alone.

This is also an area in which parents need to exercise flexibility about when, where, how often and in what ways they spend time with their children. If parents live near each other such flexibility is easier. If this is not the case, more creative thinking about how to apportion time as the children get older is helpful.

As a child's development is not static, so parental thinking and understanding must develop about how the different family relationships must also adapt. This is another reflection of the fact that divorce is a process, rather than an event.

Please also turn to Chapter 6 for more discussion of some of the pitfalls and difficulties in continued contact between children and parents who live apart.

(B) Coping with Less Money

Unless one or both of the parents subsequently forms a long-term relationship with someone on a higher income, the likelihood is that the divorced families will be surviving on scarcer resources. Two households are more expensive than one. There may also be additional expenses, such as travel costs to maintain contact or costs incurred on the contact visits themselves. Child-care costs may also be a new essential expense.

Having to change living standards is a shock and it is usually unexpected. Children can exacerbate this, for they understandably react adversely to having less of what they had before. They feel they are being punished for something they did not do.

Indeed, if there is significant economic loss sustained over a long period, and the quality of the children's lives and education suffers over such periods, there is more chance that they will be adversely affected. However, if the economic slide is not significant or long-sustained, and if the changes are not major, most children, together with their parents, will adjust to their more straitened circumstances.

14

THE EMOTIONAL AFTERMATH OF DIVORCE

(A) Anniversaries, Birthdays, Christmas

'The first time is the hardest' is a saying all divorced people should learn. Each first anniversary of any significant event formerly shared (wedding anniversaries, for instance, or anniversaries of parental deaths), each first birthday spent apart (whether your own or your children's), each first Christmas or holiday spent alone or without your former spouse is likely to be the most difficult. The ensuing ones are normally not as hard.

These ensuing anniversaries become easier in part because new routines displace old ones. For this reason it is very important to substitute past rituals with new ones. For instance, Christmas can be marked by spending it in a different place. Children's birthdays can become routinely celebrated twice – once with one parent, once with the other. Your own birthday can be marked in a different but satisfying way from the way it was in the past, if you choose to do so.

In this way new routines and expectations around significant events can be developed. This both eases the pain of letting go of the past and also carries the message that there is a new way to live in the future.

Nevertheless, anniversaries are particularly hard at first. Some societies have rituals to mark the first anniversaries of sad events as well as of happy ones. This is a way of acknowledging that there is a real difficulty in experiencing sad anniversaries. It should be expected and acknowledged that this is so, both for yourself as the adult and especially for your children, who may not have the wisdom or words to express their sad and troubling feelings. Just as rituals are important as acknowledgements, so are words. It would probably be wise both to expect sadness and also to state for your children that this is the case.

Moving on is equally important. Planning in advance what to do differently this year for your child's birthday, or how and with whom you want to celebrate yours, can help, as can letting your children help in the new celebrations. Again, the message they will receive is that it is possible to build a new life, with new sources of pleasure.

However, celebrations and rituals also underscore an important fact. When there are children involved, you are never free of your former spouse. To think otherwise is naive and will leave you constantly frustrated, even enraged. Rather than ending the relationship, divorce leads a couple into a long process of attenuation and change in a necessarily continuing relationship. There will be a relationship between parents as long as there are children, with decreasing frequency and intensity after they leave home, and again at family occasions (for example, weddings, births and funerals).

Divorce needs to become an emotional distancing, as the reality is it is never really complete, at least if there are children. Anger, bitterness and intense resentment are negative but strong ties which keep couples together, even when divorced. Emotional distancing rather than cut-off is the realistic aim, therefore, to enable both spouses to move on and to help their children to adjust. By this we mean being able to achieve a state so that the behaviour of your ex-spouse, so long as it does not adversely affect your children's health, safety and security, or the security, nature and quality of your relationship with them, makes little real difference to your own individual stability and happiness.

Implied in this is that the expectation that you can become good, or as some people hope, even best friends with your ex-spouse is not usually achievable or appropriate. It is also not realistic. The reasons for the relationship breakdown rarely change when the relationship actually ends. As we have seen in Chapter 1 and Section 4, children want their parents to remain married, and even despite remarriages and other incontrovertible evidence to the contrary they continue to wish for this. Watching parents strive for intimacy with one another after divorce can be disturbing and confusing for children. 'If you get on so well, why did you and Daddy (or Mummy) divorce?' is the question they will continue to ask.

As they fantasise about a reconciliation certain things can actually be deeply upsetting to children, such as lack of clear boundaries around new families; for instance, the parent living apart expecting to share Sunday lunch with the rest of the family, or unexpectedly turning up and setting out school clothes in the morning. Children can adjust to living in two separate but equal households, but they cannot do so if these households are not sufficiently or predictably separate.

The wish to remain very close to former spouses reflects more about the difficulty of ending a once intimate relationship than about helping the children. The honesty needed to acknowledge this is difficult, but very important.

(B) Styles of Parenting – Post-divorce

Just as a family during and after divorce goes through cycles of instability, then adjustment, followed by disequilibrium, so too does the path of post-divorce parenting. As we have seen, family members, especially divorced parents, are often interdependent, although they may have little or no direct interaction. From an emotional point of view, children do not lose parents after divorce, even if they lose contact with them.

One way of classifying post-divorce parenting is as follows:

(i) *no contact*: when one parent has no contact with the children, who live with the other parent;
(ii) *parallel parenting*: when parents do not talk to each other but the parent who lives apart maintains frequent contact with the children;
(iii) *regular and periodic but infrequent contact*: when the parent who does not live with them maintains regular, periodic though infrequent contact and such contact increases on special occasions or as a result of problems with the children;
(iv) *co-parenting*: where children spend at least 30 per cent of their time with the parent who lives apart.

If at all possible, co-parenting is preferable for children, with parallel parenting being next choice. There are exceptions to this. If there has been abuse, violence or neglect, or if there is any danger to the child from having contact, then clearly the position is different. Any contact in these circumstances would need to be considered very carefully. And co-parenting with high levels of conflict is also not good for children.

Having no contact usually has strong negative consequences. Sometimes these only show up in the longer term. Especially for younger children, lack of contact is almost inevitably interpreted as a rejection, even if explained otherwise. As children get older the prolonged effects of little or no contact begin to tell. In adolescence many children want to resume contact with their absent parent, or if contact has been sporadic and/or unpredictable not to see him or her at all. According to current research, lack of contact with their fathers is especially problematic with boys, as they move into adolescence without experiencing consistently good male role models. Such an absence of male role models for girls is also linked to difficulty later on in forming their own relationships.

A co-operative relationship between divorced parents has a positive impact on how a family functions following divorce. If two households maintain clear and consistent characteristics the children learn to switch from one situation to the other without major psychological disruption, even if those characteristics are markedly different. It is like the phenomenon, familiar to many parents (particularly of teenage children), of children using one jargon and accent at school, and adjusting to another accent and vocabulary at home.

However, a co-operative parenting relationship may be difficult to achieve. The best interests of parents and children may not always coincide. Co-parental communication is an area in which there is a great deal of confusion. We do not have much information yet about norms and options of this style. But as co-parenting grows, so will our knowledge about its strengths and pitfalls. For the moment it looks the most promising parenting style for children of divorce.

Role models for divorced parents to judge what is normal or common behaviour in unfamiliar situations are not readily available. This makes it difficult for parents to judge their efforts against the experience of others in comparable situations. For instance, divorced parents may attend occasions such as school functions or special occasions together with their children, but may hide this information from disapproving family and friends. The net effect is that they would not know whether such behaviour is common among families such as theirs.

For divorced people themselves, as well as for their families and friends, the confusion about what is 'right' and what is 'wrong' in relation to their children can be overwhelming. Also what may be 'right' when a child is 6 may not be 'right' when the child is 16. For some parents, despite ambivalent or even negative feelings for each other, some emotional attachment continues and it can be difficult to separate out continuing attachment from necessary co-parental co-operation over children. There can easily be hidden agendas; again, honesty with yourself is important in looking at motivations.

The rules or expectations for dealing with normal points of transition for families, which includes divorced families (such as marriages, births, deaths and separations) are in a period of flux.

This is clearly true for families following divorce. At times of transition children are particularly vulnerable. Moreover, children's emotional needs change over their life cycle just as their physical ones do. Both parents, even though separated, need to be sensitive to these to be able to co-operate over them. This is another way divorced parents keep having to be connected through divorce.

The *immediate* impact of divorce on children has been outlined in Chapter 6. But for some children there is a *'sleeper'* effect, with the impact of divorce and loss only hitting them years later, for instance in adolescence and affecting later school performance and when they come to form relationships of their own. It should be noted that this delayed impact may equally arise from the parents' poor relationship prior to divorce, or from adverse factors arising as a consequence of the divorce and occurring as the children grow up.

Resources within the extended family, school, church and community can often offset problems, providing support of both a practical and emotional kind. A list of organisations offering help appears in the Recommended Reading List (*see pages 179–181*).

(C) Step-parenting – An Overview

Recently available figures (General Household Survey 1991, published 1993), tell us that over one million children in the UK are growing up in a full-time step-family, with another million as members of a part-time step-family. Furthermore, over half (52 per cent) of all full-time step-families have at least one child of their own.

The emotional and practical issues in forming and coalescing as a step-family are complicated. They also differ for each person involved. For example, a step-family may look and feel very different from the standpoint of a step-mother compared with that of a step-child. The number of people involved in each step-family, as well as the numerous family patterns, make for complexity and diversity.

These issues also need to be seen against a background of powerful myths about step-families. Three common myths in the step-family landscape are:

1. the myth of the 'reconstitution' of the nuclear family even though nuclear and step-families are not the same – i.e., the step-family is not a re-creation of the nuclear family;
2. the myth of instant love or instant adjustment;
3. the myth of the wicked step-mother or step-father.

Many adults who remarry or cohabit after divorce strive to achieve the impossible. They want a problem-free nuclear family. New beginnings demand a recognition of the myths and fantasies about step-families, so that the construction of a happy step-family occurs realistically.

In practice this means:

— continuation of co-parenting with the former spouse while resolving the emotional and practical issues of divorce;
— recognition by all parties that the parent/child bond precedes that of remarriage or repartnership.

To assimilate new partners into a new step-family needs time and space. The power of myths attached to step-families often leads, for instance, to step-mothers trying too hard to avoid being mistaken for the wicked step-mother of children's stories. Step-fathers (and there are currently seven times more full-time step-fathers than step-mothers) may rush in, filled with guilt about separating from their own children, and try to take charge immediately. A step-father may also be seen as, and see himself as, a 'rescuer' of fatherless, potentially disturbed children. In their turn, step-children may resent and act out that resentment at being asked to participate in a new 'family' not of their choosing, and which does not yet feel at all comfortable to them.

(D) Characteristics of Step-families

Step-families differ from biological two-parent families in several ways:

— all step-family members have experienced loss: that of the original family;
— all members enter step-families with past family histories, now not only of their childhoods but also of previous marriages/partnerships;
— parent-child bonds precede that of the new couple's relationship;
— the biological parent, either living or deceased, has a key position;
— children often are members of two households, each with its own rules;
— the legal status of the step-parent/step-child relationship is in transition, reflecting the fast-growing variety of family forms.

(E) The Legal Status of the Step-parent/ Step-child Relationship

As we have stated in Chapter 11, upon divorce both parents retain parental responsibility for their children. That parental responsibility can be delegated to another person as necessary. This can occur, for instance, when a step-parent has the practical day-to-day care of a child when his or her natural parent is not present. This is in much the same way that such responsibility can be delegated to, for instance, a child minder, grandparent or baby-sitter.

In the past it was sometimes the case that step-parents would adopt a child following divorce, when a child had not retained an ongoing relationship with his or her other biological parent. This is now much less frequent and the law is seeking to find different mechanisms in order to recognise the increasingly multifarious family situations that exist today. The ongoing importance and role of the biological parent, whether contact is taking place or not, is emphasised.

When a step-parent does adopt a child, it is currently the case that the biological parent with whom the child lives must also adopt him or her. Save for becoming the child's guardian in the event of death, the only other way for a step-parent to obtain parental responsibility is with a residence order (*see Chapter 11*). In the light of the legal philosophy embodied in the Children Act, a court is unlikely to make such an order except in unusual circumstances, for instance where the biological parent has died or where the biological parent is frequently away from home. In other circumstances, such an order may well be regarded as unnecessary.

Reform of the law relating to adoption is currently being considered, as is the possibility of step-parents being able to obtain a parental responsibility agreement or order, giving them shared parental responsibility with the biological parents. This would clarify a step-parent's position if involved in the day-to-day care of the children. For instance, it is not difficult to foresee circumstances in which a step-parent might find him- or herself in a difficult position, such as if emergency medical treatment were required and neither biological parent was contactable. The idea behind suggesting the possibility of a parental responsibility agreement or order for step-parents is that their particular role would then be recognised.

Currently, parental responsibility agreements or orders are only available for fathers who have never been married to the mother of their children, since they do not obtain parental responsibility automatically upon a child's birth; only the mother does so in this situation.

(F) The Emotional Tasks of Step-family Development

Research has shown that several important emotional tasks are demanded if step-family life is to proceed happily and productively. The family crisis of separation and divorce can indeed be an opportunity for growth and development, rather than simply trauma and pain. Step-families represent new hope, and many achieve fulfilling new lives for their members. These emotional tasks include the following:

- Recognising and managing jealousy and loyalty conflicts: jealousy will exist, whether between children and step-parents or between step-siblings and siblings or half-siblings and siblings. There can also be conflicts of loyalty for children between step-parents and the parent with whom they do not share their main home.
- Recognition of the key role and authority of biological parents, and the change in the balance of roles in step-families for the biological parents.
- Acceptance by the step-family and extended family that changes are necessary so that new rules, traditions and habits can be negotiated and developed.
- Step-family integration in which the step-parent aims to achieve a unique role which does not usurp or compete with the other biological parent's role and is accepted by the extended family. This role, crucially, has to be validated and supported by his or her spouse.
- Integration into the step-family of new half-siblings.

Given the complexity and relative novelty of these tasks, it is not surprising that some people feel daunted, deny that these must be undergone, and then fail to negotiate them. The high casualty rate of step-families reflects this. However, those that do make it can comprise productive, happy and resilient individual family members.

From current information, the following appear to be necessary for the successful functioning of a step-family:

1 Knowledge and recognition of what to expect both emotionally and legally. This knowledge also helps to counteract the effects of step-family myths. Talking to other step-families helps, as does joining the National Step-family Association, which gives guidance and support about the special issues facing step-families.
2 The quality of both the new marriage or partnership and the parental relationship.
3 Encouragement to children (unless it is one of the very rare exceptions indicated earlier) to continue to relate to both biological parents.
4 A genuine attempt at non-hostile and civil relationships between all the adults involved in parenting.
5 The allocation of plenty of time, energy and patience for he formation of a functioning step-family.
6 Tolerance over names and naming, so that these are not imposed prematurely on children (e.g., calling step-father 'dad' or step-mother 'mum') and are chosen freely and over time by the children themselves.
7 The speedy settlement of any legal issues (financial maintenance issues, for example).

(G) Legal Issues following Divorce

From time to time, even following divorce, issues may arise which cannot be dealt with by agreement. In such cases a parent may consider commencing a legal process, or at the very least finding out more about what the legal position would be over a particular problem. While the aim should be to deal with as many disputes as possible by agreement or through mediation, it cannot be assumed that this can always be achieved. Therefore, a parent may want to apply to court for one of the orders discussed in Chapter 11. The following issues may also occur as the family following divorce matures, and may call for legal advice or intervention.

(1) Travel Abroad and Obtaining Passports

When there is no residence order in that parent's favour, it is a criminal offence for a parent to take a child out of the UK without the consent of the other parent or the court. If a parent does have a residence order, he or she is allowed to take a child out of the UK for a period of less than one month without the other parent's consent.

While in practical terms it is to be hoped that parents will generally discuss arrangements for holidays with each other, it is also a legal requirement. If for any reason one parent does not agree that such a trip abroad would be in a child's best interests, or if he or she is concerned about the child's safe return, that parent can make an application to the court to determine whether the trip should take place or not.

Currently either parent can obtain a passport for a child without the other parent's consent, unless there is a residence order or a prohibited steps order dealing with the particular point (*see Chapter 12*). The Passport Agency have been reviewing their policy in this area and it is therefore advisable to seek specific confirmation of the current legal position if this becomes an issue.

Finally, if a parent wishes to take a child to live permanently outside England and Wales, the other parent's consent or the consent of the court must be obtained. In the absence of a parent's consent, the court will consider whether it is in the child's best interests for such a permanent move, taking into consideration the proposed arrangements and also the child's current circumstances.

(2) Change of Surname

Neither parent, nor indeed any other person, can change a child's surname without the written consent of every person with parental responsibility or without leave of the court. Changing a child's surname is obviously a very emotive step, since the surname may provide an important link with the parent with whom the child does not normally live, on the one hand, while changing it may express a preference to be known as the child of the step-parent, on the other.

However, the court will not consider it appropriate to change a child's surname just because it is different to that of their half- or step-siblings, nor even because the child wants it changed. Generally, therefore, in most cases the court will not sanction a change in surname.

Increasingly, children may be part of a step-family in which children do not all share the same surname. It is therefore important that any such proposal is very carefully thought through and justifiable on quite strict grounds, such as where there is no on-going relationship whatsoever with the other biological parent.

(3) What If One Parent Dies?

Following divorce, it is likely that each parent will review any will that he or she has made, since Decree Absolute within the divorce proceedings automatically changes any will insofar as it relates to the other spouse.

When children are involved, each parent may wish to consider appointing a guardian in the event of his or her death, although that appointment may not take effect until the death of both parents. In fact, the only time upon which such an appointment would take effect prior to both parents' deaths is when the parent who dies has had a residence order at the time of his or her death.

Given the crucial importance of thinking through guardianship for children, the question of these arrangements should, if at all possible, be discussed by parents together. As well as the step-parents and biological parents, it may be helpful to discuss arrangements with the extended family, and certainly with those who are going to be appointed the children's guardians.

15

LOOKING TO THE FUTURE

When the Children Act was launched in 1991, there was a great sense among those involved professionally in family law that an important change was taking place. It was the first step in what was viewed as a series of reforms of the family law system, which simplified that system and imposed upon both parents and professionals the need to consider the interests of all children involved in divorce in a more constructive and co-operative way. The new divorce law carries on this process. By simplifying the procedure for divorce, and by making it less adversarial, it is hoped that the new spirit of co-operation will gather pace.

We have tried to show in this book how a better understanding of the emotional and legal consequences of separation and divorce can help. By thinking through the consequences of decisions, and with the knowledge of what the other members of the family are going through, we hope that this will lead to the tolerance upon which any such co-operation is founded. Only then can children avoid being put 'in the middle' and be best enabled to get over the trauma of divorce in their own time. We have also tried to show that good management of the divorce process, including wise and judicious use of professionals, can limit the damage so that you and your children can emerge from it with success.

The Children Act called for a greater degree of co-operation between the professionals involved. Those involved must play their part in this, by drawing upon help *before* relationships have got to breaking point, or before events have taken over, a process which the couple involved would otherwise have been able to control more effectively.

All professionals involved in divorce will need to adapt their respective roles if their clients are to get the best out of the differing services available to them. This will require flexibility and tolerance on their part. The professionals will also have to show the same degree of co-operation which they should be encouraging in their clients.

In the long and difficult process of divorce, it is hoped that the children involved will see the degree of co-operation, both between their parents and those guiding them professionally. Perhaps this will be one good legacy for them to carry into their own adulthood: that in adversity adults *can* work together.

GLOSSARY OF TERMS AND REFERENCES

Having given a brief outline of some of the main areas of law, here are some of the common terms you may encounter.

Acknowledgement of Service Form
the form by which the Respondent (or co-respondent) acknowledges having received the divorce petition

Affidavit
a formal statement sworn on oath to be true by the person making it, usually in support of an application to the court, for example in relation to financial matters

Ancillary Relief
general term for the possible financial orders which a court can make

Answer
the formal defence to a divorce petition

Clean Break
a financial arrangement where it is agreed or ordered that the husband and wife will make no further claims against each other for capital or maintenance

Conciliation
a historical term for mediation (*see below*)

Consent Order
an order made by a court giving effect to the terms agreed between husband and wife

Contact
(formerly access) – the arrangement by which a child sees the parent, or other individual, with whom he or she does not live

Co-respondent
a person with whom the Respondent is alleged to have committed adultery. The law no longer requires that person to be named as a co-respondent in the divorce proceedings

Court Welfare Officer
a person who prepares an independent report to assist the court in deciding what arrangements would be in the best interests of the children, where there is a disputed issue relating to them. He or she will normally discuss the situation with both parties and the children themselves

Decree Absolute
the final order of the court which brings the marriage to an end

Decree Nisi
the provisional order indicating that the court is satisfied that the ground for divorce has been established

District Judge
a County Court Judge who deals with most of the divorce proceedings and usually the financial matters

Domicile
the legal relationship between an individual and a country, usually arising from residence there with the intention of making it his or her permanent home

Family Proceedings Court
the name given to the division of the Magistrates' Court which deals with family law matters

Injunction
an order by the court preventing or requiring action, usually in an emergency

Judicial Separation
a formal separation sanctioned by the court which enables the courts to make orders about money and property

Maintenance Pending Suit
temporary maintenance pending finalisation of the divorce

Matrimonial Home
any property in which a married couple live together, whether or not they own it or rent it

Mediation
the process in which trained independent mediators try to help a couple reach agreement about arrangements to be made for children, and sometimes finances

Parental Responsibility
where married, both parents of a child have joint parental responsibility for that child before, during and after divorce or separation. It is all of the rights, duties and responsibilities which by law a parent of a child has in relation to that child

Periodical Payments
maintenance

Petition
the document by which a divorce or judicial separation is applied for

Petitioner
the person who applies for a divorce or judicial separation

Prayer
the part of the petition which asks the court to make orders in favour of the Petitioner

Prohibited Steps Order
an order prohibiting specific steps in relation to a child, for example a change of surname or removal from the jurisdiction

Property Adjustment Order
an order that a husband and wife should transfer property to the other

Residence Order
an order dealing with the arrangements about with whom a child is to live

Request for Directions
application to the court for a Decree Nisi

Respondent
the other spouse upon whom the divorce or judicial separation proceedings are served

Service
the process by which court documents are formally sent to the party they are addressed to (usually via their solicitor)

Specific Issue Order
an order determining a specific issue relating to a child; for example, an educational dispute or an issue over medical treatment

Statement of Arrangements
the form which has to be sent to the court with the petition if there are children involved, which sets out the arrangements proposed for those children when the divorce takes place. This should be agreed by the husband and wife in advance and signed by both of them if agreed.

RECOMMENDED READING LIST

Coping with Divorce

Ahrons, C. R. and Rodgers, R. H., *Divorced Families: Meeting the Challenge of Divorce and Remarriage* (W. W. Norton)

Ambrose, P., Harper J. and Pemberton, R., *Surviving Divorce: Men Beyond Marriage* (Harvester/Wheatsheaf)

Berman, C., *Adult Children of Divorce Speak Out about Growing Up with and Moving Beyond Parental Divorce* (Simon and Schuster)

Burghes, L., *Lone Parent and Family Disruption: The Outcomes for Children* (Family Policy Studies Centre)

Burgoyne, J., Ormrod, R. and Richards, M., *Divorce Matters* (Penguin)

Mitchell, A., *Coping with Separation and Divorce* (Chambers)

Street, E., *Counselling for Family Problems* (Counselling in Practice Series)

Wallerstein, J. and Blakeslee, S., *Second Chances: Men, Women and Children a Decade after Divorce* (Bantam)

Relationships

Litvinoff, S., *The Relate Guide to Better Relationships* (Vermilion)

—, *The Relate Guide to Starting Again: How to Learn from the Past to Give You a Better Future* (Vermilion)

Martyns, E., *Second Time Around: How Divorce Affects Future Relationships* (Optima)

Reibstein, J., *Love Life: How to Make Your Relationship Work* (Fourth Estate)

Reibstein, J. and Richards, M., *Sexual Arrangements: Marriage, Monogamy, and Affairs* (Mandarin)

Vaughan, D., *Uncoupling: How Relationships Come Apart* (Methuen)

Wallerstein, J. and Blakeslee, S., *The Good Marriage, How and Why Love Lasts* (Bantam)

The Post-divorce Family and Step-families

Aleksander, T., *His, Hers, Theirs: A Financial Handbook for Stepfamilies* (STEPFAMILY Publications)

Atkin, E. and Rubin, E., *Part-time Father: The Essential Guide that Offers Help and Understanding to Every Divorced Father* (Signet)

Burns, C., *Step-Motherhood: How to Survive without Feeling Frustrated, Left Out or Wicked* (Piatkus)

Collins, S., *Step-Parents and their Children* (Human Horizons Series, Souvenir Press)

Inglis, R., *The Good Step-Parents Guide* (Grafton Books)

Marshall, P., *Cinderella Revisited: How to Survive Your Stepfamily without a Fairy Godmother* (The British Psychological Society)

Newman, M., *Stepfamily Realities* (New Harbinger Publications)

Robinson, M., *Family Transformation through Divorce and Remarriage* (Tavistock/Routledge)

Robinson, M. and Smith, D., *Step by Step: Focus on Stepfamilies* (Harvester/Wheatsheaf)
Smith, D., *Stepmothering* (Harvester/Wheatsheaf)

Children and Divorce

Ayalon, O. and Flasher, A., *Chain Reaction: Children and Divorce* (Jessica Kingsley)
Burgoyne, J., *Breaking Even: Divorce, Your Children and You* (Penguin)
Burret, J., *To and Fro Children: A Guide to Successful Parenting after Divorce* (Thorsons)
Hooper, A., *Divorce and Your Children* (Robson Books)
McCredie, G. and Horrox, A., *Voices in the Dark: Children and Divorce* (Unwin Paperbacks)
Swan-Jackson, A., *Caught in the Middle: Teenagers Talk about their Parents' Divorce* (Piccadilly Press)
Tugendhat, J., *What Teenagers Can Tell Us about Divorce and Stepfamilies* (Bloomsbury)

Legal Issues

Black, J., Bridge, J. and Bond, T., *A Practical Approach to Family Law* (Blackstone Press)
Garlick, H., *The* Which? *Guide to Divorce* (Consumers' Association and Hodder & Stoughton)
The Norton Rose M5 Group, *Humphreys' Family Proceedings* (FT Law & Tax)
Salter, D. (ed), *Pensions and Insurance on Family Breakdown* (Jordan & Sons)

Mediation

Fisher, T., *The National Family Mediation Guide to Separation and Divorce* (Vermilion)

Books for Children about Separation and Divorce – kindly supplied by the Cambridge Family and Divorce Centre

Krasny Brown, Laurene, and Brown, Marc, *Dinosaurs Divorce*, age 5–8 (Collins)

Osman, Trudy and Carey, Joanna, *Where Has Daddy Gone?* age 5–8 (Heinemann)

Grunsell, Angela, *Let's Talk about Divorce*, age 8–12 (Aladdin Books)

Bryant Mole, Karen, *What's Happening? Splitting up*, age 8–12 (Wayland)

Fine, Anne, *Madam Doubtfire*, age 9+ (Penguin Books)

Blume, Judy, *It's Not the End of the World*, age 10–13 (Pan Piper)

Danziger, Paula, *The Divorce Express*, age 10–13 (Pan Piper)

Evensen Lazo, Caroline, *The Facts about Divorce*, age 10+ (Simon & Schuster)

Nystrom, Carolyn, *Mike's Lonely Summer: a Child's Guide Through Divorce*, age 10+ (Lion Publishing plc)

Books about re-marriage and new partners – kindly supplied by the Cambridge Family and Divorce Centre

Boyd, Lizi, *The Not So Wicked Stepmother*, age 3–7 (Puffin Books)

Leach, Norman and Brown, Jane, *My Wicked Stepmother*, age 5–8 (Julia MacRae Books)

McAfee, Annalena and Brown, Anthony, *The Visitors Who Came to Stay*, age 5–8 (Hamish Hamilton)

Drescher, Joan, *My Mother's Getting Married*, age 4–8 (Methuen)

Grunsell, Angela, *Let's Talk about Stepfamilies*, age 7+ (Aladdin Books)

Fine, Anne, *Goggle Eyes*, age 10+ (Penguin Books)

Danziger, Paula, *It's an Aardvark–Eat–Turtle World*, age 10–13 (Pan Piper)

Fine, Anne, *Step by Wicked Step* (Penguin Books)

USEFUL ADDRESSES

Association of Family Therapy
c/o Pauline Matthews, Admin. Sec.
18 Winnipeg Drive
Lakeside, Cardiff CF2 6ET

The British Association for Counselling
37a Sheep Street
Rugby EV21 3BX
01788 78328

British Psychological Society
St Andrews House
48 Princess Road East
Leicester LE1 7DR

Child Poverty Action Group
1–5 Bath Street
London EC1V 9PY
0171 253 3406
Fax: 0171 490 0561

Child Support Agency
Great Northern Tower
Great Victoria Street
Belfast BT2 7AD
0345 133 133 (main line)
Fax: 0345 132 007

The Children's Society
Edward Rudolf House
69–85 Margery Street
London WC1X 0JL
0171 837 4299
Fax: 0171 837 0211

Citizens' Advice Bureaux (CAB)
Address in your local telephone directory

Family Mediators Association
PO Box 2028
Hove
East Sussex BN3 3HU
01273 747 750 (and fax)

FOCUS (Forum for Occupational Counselling and Unemployment Services)
Northside House
Mount Pleasant
London EN4 9EB
0181 441 9300

Institute of Family Therapy
24–32 Stephenson Way
London NW1 2HX
0171 391 9150
Fax: 0171 391 9169

Men's Centre (for men who are violent to women)
0171 267 8713

National Children's Bureau
8 Wakley Street
London EC21V 7QE
0171 278 9441

National Council for One Parent Families
255 Kentish Town Road
London NW5 2LX
0171 267 1361
Fax: 0171 482 4851

National Family Mediation
9 Tavistock Place
London WC1H 9SN
0171 383 5993
Fax: 0171 383 5994

One-plus-One: The Marriage and Partnership Research Charity
14 Theobalds Road
London WC1X 8PF
0171 831 5261

Parentline-OPUS (Organisation for Parents Under Stress)
Rayfa House
57 Hart Road
Thundersley
Essex SS7 3PD
01268 757 077

Parent Network
444–46 Caversham Road
London NW5 2DS
0171 485 8535

Relate
11 Little Church Street
Rugby CV21 3AW
01788 565 675 (no fax)

The Samaritans
Address and phone number in local phone directory

The Stepfamily Association
3rd floor, Chapel House
18 Hatton Place
London EC1N 8RU
0171 209 2460 (office)
0171 209 2464 (counselling)

Women's Aid Federation (England)
PO Box 391
Bristol BS99 7WS
01272 420 611

38–48 Crwys Road
Cardiff CF2 4NN

11 St Colne Street
Edinburgh EH3 6AG

143a University Street
Belfast BT7 1HP

Working Mothers' Association
77 Holloway Road
London N7 8JZ
0171 700 5771

INDEX